MAI GOODNESS

Vietnamese Home Cooking: Spirits, Traditions, and Foods to Invite the Ancestors Home

MAI DONOHUE

JULIA CALIFANO

Mai Donohue
10 Woodward Avenue
Barrington, RI 02806
Phone: 401-245-3770
Email: mai@maigoodness.com

Julia P. Califano
151 Mathewson Road
Barrington, RI 02806
Phone: 401-247-0271
Email: jpcalifano2@gmail.com

Visit our website at **www.StillwaterPress.com** for more information.

First Stillwater River Publications Edition
Library of Congress Control Number: 2019920954

ISBN: 978-1-950339-75-4

1 2 3 4 5 6 7 8 9 10

Written by Mai Donohue and Julia Califano.

Published by Stillwater River Publications, Pawtucket, RI, USA.

Publisher's Cataloging-In-Publication Data
(Prepared by The Donohue Group, Inc.)

Names: Donohue, Mai, author. | Califano, Julia, author.
Title: Mai goodness : Vietnamese home cooking : spirits, traditions, and foods to bring the ancestors home / Mai
      Donohue [and] Julia Califano.
Description: First Stillwater River Publications edition. | Pawtucket, RI, USA : Stillwater River Publications, [2021]
Identifiers: ISBN 9781950339754
Subjects: LCSH: Cooking, Vietnamese. | Vietnam--Social life and customs. | LCGFT: Cookbooks.
Classification: LCC TX724.5.V5 D66 2020 | DDC 641.59597--dc23

The views and opinions expressed in this book are solely those of the author(s)
and do not necessarily reflect the views and opinions of the publisher.

In Vietnam, the tradition of telling stories
while preparing and sharing food with friends
and family is a way to honor the past
and look ahead to the future.

In writing this cookbook,
we hope to pass that tradition
on to the next generation.

Mai's daughter Maura lights incense
at the graves of her ancestors.

Contents

Main Dishes

Banquet Dishes

Side Dishes

Desserts

Introduction

Music, food, family and story telling are important elements of the Vietnamese tradition. The men working in the fields and the women cooking in the courtyards often pass the time exchanging gossip and telling folk tales. One of the stories Mai Donohue frequently tells her children when they complain about the food she serves is the story of **The King and the Rock Soup.**

Once upon a time there was a King who suffered from a sickness called "Nothing Tastes Good." All day long he ate, but everything tasted the same: like sawdust. The King became so depressed that his wives and chefs became concerned for his health and searched for the most exotic specialty foods in the Kingdom. Days, weeks and months passed, but everything they found still tasted like sawdust, and the King grew increasingly angry.

"Find food that suits my taste or...off with your heads!" the King shouted, and the army went out in search of the most exotic ingredients, and the cooks prepared hundreds of meals in different ways, but nothing helped. The King got more depressed, and everyone began to fear for his life.

One day, the King was sitting in his tower and saw a poor farmer walking by the castle and noticed that the farmer was smiling.

"Why are you smiling?" the King called to the farmer. "How can you be content when you are poor and have so little to eat while I am rich and have everything to eat but nothing tastes good?"

"What is your secret?" the King demanded.

"Have you never eaten Rock Soup?" the farmer asked, bowing low.

"Never heard of it," the King answered, "but you can make me some right now."

"I would love to, my King," the farmer said with another bow, "but Rock Soup can only be prepared in the right place at the right time."

"Where is the right place and when is the right time?" the King demanded.

"The first of the month at my humble home," the farmer replied.

"I can't wait that long!" the King shouted, but the farmer bowed low again and insisted that the soup could only be prepared properly in the right place at the right time, and the King finally agreed to be patient.

"When you come to my home," the farmer added, "you must walk there and not bring your men. Otherwise, the magic will not work."

The King had never had to wait for anything in his life and was furious but finally agreed.

"This had better be good or you and your whole family will lose your heads!" the King threatened.

When the first of the month finally arrived, the King left behind his entourage in the castle and walked alone to the poor farmer's cottage. When he arrived late in the afternoon, there was a big pot of water boiling on the open fire, and inside the pot was a large rock. The King was very excited, but the farmer told him that the soup was not yet ready.

After several hours, the King complained about being hungry, and the farmer's wife served him some tea. Several more hours passed, and the King complained again that he was hungry.

"The magic rock soup takes a very long time to cook," the farmer tried to explain. "If I serve the soup too soon it will not cure your sickness. However, my wife can prepare some simple dishes for you while you wait."

The farmer's wife brought the King small dishes of a vegetable and tofu stir fry, steamed rice and fish sauce, and the King ate greedily.

"What are these dishes called?" the King asked when he had finished eating. "I have never tasted anything so good."

"It is just the fish sauce we ferment, the simple vegetables we grow in the courtyard and rice from the fields," the farmer answered, and the King suddenly understood and laughed.

"You are very brave and very wise," the King said. "You made me walk alone all this way and wait while the rock cooked in the boiling water, which was never going to become soup, but I became so hungry that I could finally appreciate whatever I was served. You have taught me a valuable lesson, and from now on, I will eat to live, not live to eat."

The farmer's family became the King's personal cooks, and the King went on long daily walks, ate only the vegetables and foods that were fresh and readily available, never complained again and sat down to eat only when he was hungry.

Cooking is an important part of my earliest memories of childhood in Thong an Ninh, a rural hamlet south of Quang Ngai in the central highlands of Vietnam. Thong an Ninh, is a town not far from the 17th parallel, which would eventually become the dividing line between North and South Vietnam, and my mother married the first son of a large landowner there. I was my mother's third child, born during Ho Chi Minh's war of independence from French colonial rule, and when my younger brother was born and I was only one year old, the Viet Minh came to the village and killed all the men in the family, leaving my mother a widow at twenty-seven.

As a child I was always hungry. The Viet Minh soldiers took over our house and only gave us the scraps leftover from their meal. Everyone had to work, but by the time I was five, I was still too small to work in the rice fields, and my mother assigned me the job of taking care of my younger nieces and nephews. I learned to cook simple meals for them with salt, water, rice and sweet potato chips, and I caught the tiny crabs from the rice paddies to add protein and flavor to those meals. My younger brother Mang always complained about those crab dinners, but when he left home to join the Viet Cong, he often spent weeks in the jungle, lonely, afraid and hungry, and his hopes were kept alive by memories of those crab dinners.

After the French left Vietnam in 1954, the country was divided, and Thong an Ninh became part of South Vietnam. The South Vietnamese government was more lenient than the French or Viet Minh, and we were able to slaughter our own animals, worship ancestors on the anniversaries of their deaths and celebrate weddings and Tet, the lunar New Year. We did not have much, but those are the years I remember best: the sunrises, the sherbet-colored sky and sunsets when the farmers arrived home with heavy packets on the ends of their long, bamboo poles. On moonlit, hot summer nights when we had finished our chores, my cousin Diem and I would wander through the hamlet eavesdropping on the old men and listening to the women tell stories.

On the anniversaries of our ancestors' deaths, my mother's first duty was to care for the family altar, clean the graves and prepare for the celebration. It was an honor to be invited to help with the cooking, and my mother would invite most of the neighbor women, who worked until the wee hours of the morning, killing the ducks, plucking the chickens and quartering the pig while their daughters hauled water, cleaned the vegetables and washed the dishes. It was hard work, but everyone took pleasure in the communal effort, and I can still remember the smell of the barbecue smoke from meats cooking over a hot charcoal fire and dripping the marinade of freshly harvested ginger, lemon grass, curry and fish sauce. When I close my eyes, I still see tray after tray of small dishes and sweet rice in front of the ancestors' altar and soup bowls on the table next to green papaya salad covered with toasted rice crackers.

I also see my mother, wearing her best Ao Dai, kneeling in front of the altar and holding up three burning sticks of incense. Bowed low, she spoke softly to invite the spirits of the ancestors to come home. The oldest men were the first served, followed by the younger men and then the women too old to share in the cooking. The women and girls who did the cooking were served last.

Mai wearing a traditional Vietnamese Ao Dai in the Thong an Ninh courtyard.

Back row, left to right: Mai's sister-in law Thua, brother Than, sister Can, younger brother Mang, sister-in-law Dong.

Front row: Mai and her mother.

For the first fifteen years of my life, I knew almost nothing of the world beyond Thong an Ninh, but the deprivations of war and a brutal marriage at the age of thirteen eventually led me to escape and disappear in the crowded streets of Saigon. There I worked as a maid to wealthy families, and I met cooks who had learned French, Indian and Chinese cuisine as well as the cooking of both North and South Vietnam. Because I loved to cook, they encouraged me to cook with them, and I learned very fast. They also took me to the markets and taught me how to pick out the freshest fish and ripest vegetables and fruit.

While working In Saigon, I met Brian Donohue, a young American Naval Officer, and quickly cooked my way into his heart. When we married and came to the United States in 1970, however, Brian wanted me to become American, learn to drive a car, shop in a supermarket and cook American food. When I occasionally was homesick, I would shut all the windows and doors so that the neighbors would not get wind of my Vietnamese country cooking and its pungent aromas, but when four Vietnamese boys came to live with us after the fall of Saigon in 1975, they begged me to cook Vietnamese food for them, and soon the smells of my cooking spread through the neighborhood and I began hosting Vietnamese luncheons for my friends.

When I first invited Julia Califano for lunch, she asked for a copy of my recipes, but although I had lived in America for twenty years, none of the recipes were written down, and it was difficult for me to write in English. Julia offered to watch me cook and write down the ingredients and directions so that my children would someday be able to cook Vietnamese food, and we spent many wonderful hours together cooking and telling stories. After more than a year of effort, we had a book of recipes for simple foods found in the open market stalls, regional specialties and traditional banquet dishes, and although the list of ingredients might seem intimidating and would take many hands and hours of chopping in Thong An Ninh, most of the recipes are generous salad platters with a few, savory additions, and the chopping can be done in minutes with a food processor. While cooking, I told Julia the stories from my childhood, which we decided to include with the recipes, and Julia and I were so pleased with our collaboration that we spent another year tracking down agents and publishers to help us get the book published. We finally got in the door of a major publisher in New York but were eventually turned away, so we printed out copies of the cookbook on the computer and gave them away to friends and family.

Whenever one of my children graduated from school or had something special to celebrate, they asked me to prepare a traditional Vietnamese banquet for their friends, and word of those parties and the cookbook spread.

Eventually, however, I decided to finish the education cut short by war and circumstance and went back to school, graduated from college and got a job in the Barrington (RI) schools where I used my experiences to encourage students struggling to learn. Cooking, however, remains my passion and connection with family, friends and the past. My children are grown now, married with children of their own. They live in California, Arizona, New York and Rhode Island, but they always come back when they can and sit around our dining room table, sharing a home-cooked meal and their own favorite tales and memories.

— **Mai Donohue & Julia Califano**

The funeral procession for Mai's mother through the rice fields.

Mourners gather to invite the
ancestors home with offerings of
food, flowers, and incense.

Appetizers

Some of the most distinctive Southeast Asian dishes can be served as appetizers or as main dishes. Goi Cuon, Cha Gio, Banh Bao, Wontons and Eggrolls are some of the most popular and best known Vietnamese dishes, and although they are usually served in restaurants as appetizers and as snack foods by street vendors, they can be combined with salad platters in home cooking and make a tasty and elegant meal for family or guests. They are time consuming to prepare the first time, but guests will enjoy helping in the final preparations, and most can be made ahead of time and refrigerated or frozen.

FRESH SPRING ROLLS

GOI CUON in Vietnamese, or NIMH CHA in Cambodian

1 lb. medium, uncooked shrimp,
  peeled and deveined

½ lb. of rice stick noodles

1 head leaf lettuce (Boston or
  Romaine) or other leafy greens

½ lb. bean sprouts

1 medium cucumber, sliced into
  matchsticks

1 medium carrot, peeled and
  shredded

½ cup fresh mint leaves

½ cup fresh basil leaves

½ cup fresh cilantro leaves

5 cups water

1 tsp. salt

1 8 oz. package circular rice papers
  (about 8 ½" diameter)

sesame oil

APPETIZER/MAIN DISH
SERVES 10-15   MAKES 30-35 GOI CUON

1. Bring ½ cup of water to a boil and add the shrimp. Cook for 2 minutes until shrimp turns pink. Run the shrimp under cold water, drain, peel and cut in half lengthwise. (Or you can buy cooked and cleaned shrimp and cut it in half)

2. In a large pot, bring 5 cups of water to a boil. Add 1 tsp. salt and the rice stick noodles. Cook for 3-4 minutes. Drain, rinse in cool water, cut into 2" lengths and set aside.

3. Wash the vegetables and slice the cucumbers in matchstick slices. Chop the lettuce and mix with the cucumbers, bean sprouts, mint, basil and cilantro. (The bean sprouts can also be soaked in hot water in a large bowl and then drained to soften to make it easier to roll the goi cuon.)

To prepare the rice paper wrappers:

1. Put warm water and 1 tsp. sugar in a pie plate or shallow bowl. Submerge the rice papers one at a time in the water and then set aside on a flat surface to soften (You can soften 5 or 6 rice papers at a time).

2. When the papers are soft and pliable, fold the bottom edge of the rice paper up to create a straight edge.

3. Place 1/3 cup of the vegetables, 3 shrimp halves and 1 tbsp. of rice noodles on the bottom edge of the wrapper. Fold the sides of the wrapper over the filling and roll up tightly like an eggroll.

To keep the goi cuon from sticking together, rub sesame oil on your hands and roll the goi cuon in your hands before storing on a flat surface and covered with plastic wrap.

Serve with **peanut dipping sauce (p.22), nuoc cham (spicy fish sauce; p.21),** and **ground peanuts.** Dip the roll in a sauce and then in the ground peanuts before eating.

VIETNAMESE SPRING ROLLS

CHA GIO (CHA YO)

5 oz. bean thread or Chinese vermicelli noodles

1 cup wood ears

½ lb. uncooked shrimp

1 lb. ground pork

12 oz. fresh mushrooms

1 large onion

2 cloves garlic

2 eggs

½ tsp. pepper

½ tsp. seasoned salt

2 tbsp. fish sauce

I package rice papers*

1 tsp. sugar

vegetable or peanut oil for frying

APPETIZER/MAIN DISH   SERVES 15-20
MAKES 35-40 MEDIUM CHA GIO

1. Soak the bean thread or noodles in hot water for 3-5 minutes. Drain, cool and chop to bite sized pieces.

2. Soak the wood ears in boiling water for 15 minutes. Drain and grind in a food processor or chop fine.

3. One at a time in the food processor, grind the shrimp, onions, garlic, and mushrooms.

4. Put all the ground ingredients in a large bowl. Add the fish sauce, the seasonings, and the eggs. Mix all the ingredients thoroughly with your hands.

5. Put warm water and 1 tsp. sugar in a pie tin (The sugar will help the cha gios to brown). Submerge the rice papers, one at a time, in the water and then set aside to let soften (You can work with 5-6 rice papers at a time). When soft, fold the bottom edge of the rice paper up to form a straight edge. Place 2 tbsp. filling on the edge. Fold over the sides and roll up tightly.

6. In an electric or regular fry pan, add about ½" of cooking oil and heat to 400 degrees. Place the cha gios in the oil and brown thoroughly on all sides. Remove to a paper towel to drain. The rice papers do not absorb much oil, so you will not have to add oil in cooking.

Serve wrapped in a fresh lettuce leaf and dipped in **nuoc cham (spicy fish sauce, p.21)** and then in **ground peanuts.** (Or serve with a **salad platter** of lettuce, shredded carrots, basil, cilantro, mint, bean sprouts and small sections of cha gio and ground peanuts and use the nuoc cham as a salad dressing.)

Rice papers come in several different sizes. The smallest are a triangle, which make a small, cocktail sized cha gio. The larger sizes are round and will hold a much longer tube of filling and, therefore, require less time cooking. If you use the larger papers, cut them with kitchen shears or a knife into bite sized pieces after cooking.

Cha gios served with nuoc cham, ground peanuts, and shredded carrots.

In Vietnam, good table manners require that some food be left on the plate at the end of each meal to signify that the host has been generous and prepared an ample number of dishes. Not understanding the Vietnamese tradition and being very fond of home-style cha gios, one of Brian Donohue's friends ate everything on his plate while dining at a Vietnamese home in Saigon. There was consternation in the kitchen, as the women prepared batch after batch of cha gios and watched them quickly disappear, but finally the young American naval officer could eat no more and, thanking his hosts profusely, left the last few cha gios on the platter.

Leftover cha gios are never a problem, however. Cha gios can be made ahead, frozen (after frying) and reheated in a 350 degree oven on a cookie sheet.

VIETNAMESE SPRING ROLLS (MEATLESS)

CHA GIO CHAY

1 lb. savory cabbage strips, chopped
fine (about 7 cups)

1 large carrot, shredded (about 2
cups)

5 oz. mushrooms, chopped

½ lb. yam or sweet potato, shredded

1 large onion, chopped fine

1 cup wood ears, soaked in boiling
water, drained and chopped

1 small (1.8 oz.) package bean
thread

½ lb. shrimp, peeled and deveined
(omit for a vegetarian dish)

2 large eggs

1 lb. fried tofu - sliced into 14
strips (available in refrigerator
section)*

cooking oil

2 tbsp. sesame oil

1 tsp. garlic salt

1 tbsp. seasoning salt

1 tsp. black pepper

3 cloves garlic, crushed with the
handle of a knife

1 package rice papers

APPETIZER/MAIN DISH   SERVES 15-20   MAKES 35-40 MEDIUM CHA GIO CHAY

1. Pour boiling water over the wood ears and let soak for 15 minutes. Drain and chop fine.

2. Cook bean thread in boiling water for 2-3 minutes. Drain and cut into bite sized pieces.

3. Grind the cleaned and deveined shrimp in a food processor.

4. Bring 4 cups of water in a large pot to a boil. Add the cabbage, carrots, and mushrooms to the boiling water. Cook and stir to blanch for 3 minutes and then drain in a colander. Squeeze out any excess liquid. Transfer the vegetables to a large bowl and add the sweet potato, onion, wood ears, bean thread, shrimp, eggs and fried tofu.

5. Add the sesame oil, garlic salt, seasoning salt, black pepper and garlic and mix all together with your hands.

6. Put hot water and 1 tsp. sugar in a pie plate. (The sugar will help with the browning of the cha gios.) Wet each rice paper with water, one at a time and then set aside to soften. (You can work with 5-6 rice papers at a time.)

7. When the rice papers are soft, fold the bottom edge to form a straight edge. Put 2 tbsp. filling on the fold. Fold each side over the filling and then roll tightly.

Put ½" cooking oil in an electric fry pan or wok and heat to 400 degrees. Brown the cha gios thoroughly on each side (about 8 minutes). Remove and drain on paper towels and then serve.

Serve with **peanut dipping sauce (p.22), nuoc cham (spicy fish sauce; p.21)** and **ground peanuts.** Or serve on top of salad greens with shredded carrots, basil, cilantro, mint, bean sprouts, ground peanuts and fish sauce.

If you cannot find fried tofu, put ½" cooking oil in fry pan and heat. Fry the tofu strips for 3-5 minutes on each side and then remove from the oil and drain on paper towels. Chop fine.

Cooking cha gios over an open fire.

STEAMED DUMPLINGS

BANH (CAKE) BAO (PURSE-SHAPED)

Ingredients for sweet dough:

1 cup milk

1 tsp. salt

½ cup sugar

3 tbsp. butter

2 eggs

2 packages dry yeast

5 cups all purpose flour (use 4 cups, if using this dough to make breakfast rolls)

1 tbsp. cooking oil

Ingredients for filling:

¾ lb. lean ground pork

3 hard-boiled eggs

½ cup wood ears

6 oz. mushrooms

½ bunch (4-5) scallions

½ lb. medium shrimp

1 small onion

1 clove garlic

1/8 tsp. fresh ground black pepper

2 tbsp. fish sauce

1 tbsp. soy sauce

aluminum foil/parchment paper

APPETIZER/MAIN DISH   SERVES 8-10
MAKES ABOUT 20 BANH BAO

For dough:

1. Heat the milk in a saucepan to lukewarm. Add the salt and sugar. Remove from the heat and add butter and allow it to melt. Cool to room temperature.

2. Put the yeast in a bowl and add the milk mixture. Do not add hot milk or you will kill the yeast action. Beat with an electric mixer and then add 2 cups of flour and continue to beat. Add the eggs and continue mixing. Add 2 more cups of flour and mix together with a wooden spoon or dough blade.

3. Put 1 cup of the flour on a smooth surface and pour the dough out onto the floured surface and knead together for 5 minutes.

4. Put 1 tbsp. cooking oil in a large bowl. Put the dough in the bowl and roll it to cover the surface with the oil to prevent sticking. Cover the bowl with a clean, dry cloth or plastic wrap and place in a warm spot to let rise for 1–1 ½ hours.

For filling:

1. Pour boiling water over the wood ears and let soak to soften for about 15-20 minutes. Grind the wood ears in a food processor or chop.

2. Grind the shrimp, mushrooms, scallions, onion and garlic separately in the food processor and then put together with the wood ears in a large bowl. Add the ground pork, the black pepper, the fish sauce and soy sauce and mix thoroughly.

3. Peel the hard-boiled eggs and cut each into eight pieces.

4. Cut the aluminum foil or parchment paper into about 20 2" squares.

5. Take a golf ball sized piece of dough and spread or roll it out into a circle of about 4" diameter. (Dough should be about 3/16" thick. It will puff up during steaming, but if it is too thin, the filling will be too heavy and break through the dough.) Place 1 ½ tbsp. filling in the center of the circle and top with 1 piece of hard-boiled egg. Bring up the sides of the dough to contain the filling and pinch and twist the top to form a purse shaped dumpling.

6. Dip the bottom of the dumpling in cooking oil to prevent sticking and place each dumpling on an aluminum foil or parchment square.

7. Put the dumplings in a steamer and steam for 10-15 minutes. Remove from the foil or parchment and serve alone or with **nuoc cham (spicy fish sauce; p.21)**.

Extra filling can be sautéed and added to an omelet, rice, or a vegetable dish.

Dumplings can be frozen after steaming and reheated by microwave or re-steaming.

Banh bao are sold by street vendors all over Saigon, but Mai's Godmother preferred the banh bao from Cholon, the twin city and Chinatown of Saigon. She would take two buses to get to Cholon and two buses back to deliver the dumplings steaming hot at Mai's door.

Ready-mix dumpling dough is available in Asian markets, but it has little flavor and is very flaky when steamed. Mai prefers this easy, sweet dough recipe, which duplicates the flavors from Cholon.

MAI'S EGG ROLLS

1 lb. ground pork (about 2 cups)

2 medium onions, chopped fine

10 large celery stalks, chopped
    (makes about 4-5 cups)

½ lb. uncooked shrimp, peeled,
    deveined and ground

4 cloves garlic

1 tbsp. cooking oil

2 cubes chicken bouillon, smashed
    into powder

¼ tsp. or more ground, black
    pepper, to taste

2 tbsp. soy sauce

1 tbsp. fish sauce

¼ tsp. seasoned salt

1 ½ cups cooking oil

1 ½-2 lb. eggroll skins (fresh, not
    frozen)

leaf lettuce for garnish

APPETIZER/MAIN DISH   SERVES 8-10
MAKES 18-20 LARGE ROLLS

1. String the celery with a knife and chop into ¼" pieces. Chop the onions into ¼" pieces. Smash the garlic with the handle of the knife and mince.

2. Peel and devein the shrimp and grind in a food processor.

3. Heat 1 tbsp. cooking oil in a large, non-stick fry pan to very hot (400 degrees). Add the garlic, then the pork and cook until thoroughly browned (about 2 minutes), stirring frequently. Add the ground shrimp and cook, stirring for another 2 minutes. Add the onion and celery and stir. Finally, add the chicken bouillon, seasoned salt and pepper and stir for another few minutes until cooked but still crunchy.

4. Turn off the heat and add the soy sauce and fish sauce. Spread the filling onto a platter to cool.

5. Heat 1 ½ cups cooking oil in a wok to 350-400 degrees. (To test, tear off a piece of eggroll skin and drop in the oil. If the oil is hot enough, the dough will bounce up to the surface immediately.)

6. Spread an eggroll skin on the counter and put ½ cup filling at one corner of the skin. Fold that corner over the filling and then fold over the two side corners to make a pocket. Roll up the eggroll and wet the final corner with water to form a seal and keep the eggroll closed while cooking.

7. Put 3 eggrolls at a time in the hot oil, with the sealed edge at the bottom. Cook for 4-5 minutes on one side and then turn and cook another 4-5 minutes on the other until golden brown. Remove from the oil and drain, propped upright, on a platter covered with paper toweling.

8. Garnish a platter with leaf lettuce and top with the eggrolls.

9. If you have leftover eggroll skins, roll them up into a cylinder and cut into ½" strips. Cook in the hot oil until golden brown, stirring to separate the strips. Serve as a snack with **sweet dipping sauce** or a **Chinese mustard sauce.**

In Vietnam, there are relatively few surnames, and although family relationships are important, many people change their names to suit their circumstances. Mai's surname at birth was Tran, her father's family name, but she changed to her mother's family name Nguyen (pronounced "Win") when she went to Saigon. Both names are extremely common in Vietnam, and because the last emperors in Vietnam were the Nguyen dynasty, many Vietnamese changed their surnames to honor the emperors, although they were not related.

The first Nguyen emperor changed his name to Gia Long in 1802 to represent the reunification of the north and south under one rule, and he moved the capital to Hue in the long and narrow, central region of the country.

Ho Chi Minh changed his name twice, as his political circumstances altered. He was also known as Ly Thuy and Nguyen Ai Quoc.

Mai has changed her name three times. The third of four children, she was originally named Can by her mother, because it rhymed with the names of her older brother and sister. Children in the same family would often be given names that rhymed or that were linked by their meanings.

In Saigon, Mai changed her name from Can, which means neat or tidy, to Ngoc Mai (pronounced Nok My), which means beautiful jade morning, because she liked both the sound and the image. When she was baptized in the Catholic church, she became Marie Mai, which she changed to Mary Mai when she became an American citizen.

WONTONS

2 cups water

½ lb. pork tenderloin (or shoulder)
    cut into cubes

¼ lb. raw shrimp, peeled and
    deveined

1 bunch of scallions, cut into 2"
    pieces

8 oz. can of water chestnuts

6 oz. fresh white mushrooms

½ tbsp. fresh ginger

2 cloves garlic

1 tbsp. fish sauce

1 tbsp. soy sauce

dash, fresh ground black pepper

2, 14 oz. packages of fresh egg roll
    or wonton wrappers

½ cup cold water

4 cups canola or corn oil

APPETIZER   SERVES 15-20   50 WONTONS

1. Bring 2 cups of water to a boil. Add mushrooms and cook for 2-3 minutes, drain and cool. Squeeze out extra water. Grind the mushrooms, ginger, garlic, water chestnuts and scallions in the food processor.

2. Grind the pork and shrimp in a food processor and add to the vegetable mixture.

3. Add the fish sauce, soy sauce and ground black pepper.

4. Lay 3-4 wonton wrappers on a cutting board (or use kitchen shears to cut egg roll wrappers into quarters).

5. Put 1 tsp. of filling in the center of the wrapper square. Wet the edges of the square with the ½ cup of cold water and fold the square across diagonally into a triangle. Seal the edges by pressing down with your fingers.

6. Heat cooking oil in a wok to 400 degrees and deep fry the wontons until golden brown. Remove the wontons from the oil and drain on a paper towel.

Wontons can be eaten cold or hot and can be reheated in a 350 degree oven on a cookie sheet.

Serve with **sweet dipping sauce (p.23).**

MARINATED TOFU or CUCUMBERS

DAU HU (TOFU) GIA VI (MARINATED)
DUA CHUOT (CUCUMBERS) GIA VI (MARINATED)

2 cloves garlic, crushed with the
    heel of a knife

2 tbsp. sugar

1 tbsp. fish sauce

3 tbsp. soy sauce

1 tbsp. sweet chili sauce

1 tsp. fresh ginger, minced

dash, crushed red pepper

4 tbsp. rice vinegar

2 tbsp. sesame oil

2 blocks of tofu, cubed, or 4 small
    cucumbers, cut into matchstick
    slices

APPETIZER OR CONDIMENT   SERVES 4-6   1 ½ CUPS

1. Mix the garlic, sugar, fish sauce, soy sauce, chili sauce, ginger, pepper, rice vinegar and sesame oil together thoroughly.

2. Cube the tofu or slice the cucumbers, leaving the skin on.

3. Pour the sauce over the tofu or cucumbers and let marinate overnight. Turn from time to time.

Serve at room temperature or chilled.

MAI'S SPICY CHICKEN WINGS

GA (CHICKEN) CANH (WING) CHIEN (FRIED) GON (CRISPY)

5 lb. chicken wings (fresh or frozen)

½ tsp. seasoned salt

½ tsp. garlic salt

¼ tsp. ground, black pepper

1 cup cooking oil

Ingredients for sauce:

1 tbsp. butter

3 tbsp. soy sauce

2 tbsp. fish sauce

1 tbsp. honey

3 tbsp. sugar

1 tsp. chili sauce or Tabasco sauce

1 tbsp. sweet chili sauce

2 cloves garlic, minced

½ tbsp. fresh ginger, peeled and minced

2 tbsp. rice vinegar

APPETIZER   SERVES 8-10   30 WINGS

1. Wash and cut off the tips of the chicken wings. Sprinkle the chicken with salt, seasoned salt and pepper and set aside for 20 minutes or longer.

2. Melt the butter in a small saucepan. Add the soy sauce, fish sauce, honey, sugar, chili sauce, Tabasco sauce, garlic, ginger and vinegar. Stir together and simmer for 5 minutes. Remove from the heat and allow to cool.

3. Heat 1 cup of cooking oil in a fry pan and fry the chicken wings for about 5 minutes on each side (10 minutes on each side, if frozen) or until crispy.*

4. Mix the chicken wings with the sauce and put on a platter to serve.

The sauce in this recipe is enough for 5 or 6 pounds of wings (there are about 6 wings to a pound), and the recipe can be doubled or tripled for a larger group. These wings are always a favorite with Mai's teenage children and their friends.

The chicken wings can also be spread in a single layer on a cookie sheet or shallow pan with a rim and baked in a 450 degree oven. Fresh wings will be crispy after baking for 10-15 minutes on each side. Frozen wings should be baked for 20 minutes on each side. For added crispness, broil for an additional 5 minutes

CONCH MEATBALLS

OC VO (CONCH) VIEN (BALL)

2 cloves garlic

1 lb. conch meat (or substitute 1 lb. shrimp)

½ lb. ground pork

3 shallots

7 medium mushrooms

1" piece of ginger, peeled

1 large egg

1 tsp. ground black pepper

3 tbsp. fish sauce

1 tbsp. butter or margarine

1 ½ cup white wine

2 tbsp. chopped chives or scallions, for garnish

APPETIZER   8-10   MAKES 40 SMALL MEATBALLS

1. Grind the conch meat (or shrimp) into very small pieces in a food processor. Remove to a bowl.

2. In the bowl of the food processor, add the garlic, shallots, mushrooms and ginger (as well as the pork, if it is not already ground) and process until all the ingredients are well ground and blended. Add the ground pork and other ingredients to the ground conch meat. Add the black pepper, egg and fish sauce and mix thoroughly.

3. Preheat the oven to 350 degrees. Form the meat mixture into small (¾") meatballs.

4. Melt 1 tbsp. of butter or margarine in a large frying pan over high heat. Add the meatballs and sauté, turning to brown (about 1 ½ minutes to a side). When finished browning, remove the meatballs to a shallow baking dish.

5. Pour the white wine into the fry pan and heat, scraping all the remaining cooking bits. Pour the wine and cooking bits over the meatballs in the baking dish and place in the 350 degree oven. Bake for 15-20 minutes, until the wine is partially absorbed in the meatballs and the liquid is bubbling.Remove the meatballs to a serving platter and garnish with the chopped chives or scallions.

These meatballs can be made ahead through the browning in the frying pan. Just before serving, pour the white wine over the meatballs and bake for 20 minutes.

Serve by themselves with toothpicks for elegant hors d'oeuvres or with **crusty French bread** to mop up the wine sauce, or make small meatball sandwiches

PICKLED RADISHES & CARROTS

CU CAI CAROT (CARROTS) VA (WITH) CAI TRANG (RADISHES) DAM CHUA (MARINATED)

1 lb. white radish roots (shaped like
a white carrot)

2-3 medium carrots

½ cup sugar

¾ cup white vinegar

1 tsp. salt

APPETIZER OR CONDIMENT   2 CUPS

1. Peel the radishes and carrots. Slice them into matchstick slices (or use a food processor).

2. Mix sugar, salt and vinegar together in a bowl. Pour over radishes and carrots and mix thoroughly to cover.

3. Cover the bowl with plastic wrap and refrigerate for several hours or over night.

4. Remove the radishes and carrots from the bowl and serve.

This is a mildly flavored but tasty condiment or appetizer. It will spice up any main dish with chicken or even hamburgers and can be used in the **banh mi Vietnamese sandwiches** to add a little crunch.

May be kept refrigerated for a week or more.

Sauces

Nuoc Cham or spicy fish sauce is always on the table for a Vietnamese meal. The basic fish sauce (nuoc mam) found bottled in the markets is derived from fermented fish (usually cuttlefish) and used to spike the flavor in most dishes as well as a dressing for fresh vegetables and salads. Shredded carrots and ground peanuts are also common condiments on the Vietnamese table, and shredded carrots are frequently floated in the nuoc cham. To serve goi cuon and cha gio, first wrap them in a lettuce leaf, dip them into the nuoc cham or peanut dipping sauce and then dip them into the ground peanuts.

Unlike Chinese women, women in Vietnam are able to inherit property and retain their maiden names after marriage. Women's intelligence, resourcefulness and tenacity are often celebrated in Vietnamese poetry and folk songs. Women have also played significant roles in the country's long history, and probably the most famous women in Vietnam history are the Trung sisters, who led a rebellion against Chinese rule from 39 to 43 AD.

Living in a rural hamlet and losing her husband when she was pregnant with her fourth child, Mai's mother struggled to maintain the land her husband had inherited as the first son. She worked in her rice fields, milled the rice, tended her fruit trees and vegetable crops, raised pigs, chickens and silk worms, spun cotton and silk thread, wove her own cloth and then dyed it a rich black for special occasions or gray for everyday, fermented her own fish sauce, prepared herbal medicines and home remedies, and even repaired her own roof thatch. Since the ancestral spirits were thought to reside in the roof rafters, repairing the roof was considered a heavy job usually reserved for the men.

Mai's mother was proud of her independence, but when Mai was eleven, her mother was forced to rent out some of her land, and there was no money left to pay the small tuition to send Mai to school. Unwilling to admit her poverty even to her daughter, Mai's mother told her that girls did not need more schooling because they would never have to support a family. What little money she had, Mai's mother used for her sons' tuitions, and she justified her decision by quoting from The Tale of Kieu:

"This we have learned: with Heaven rest all things.

Heaven appoints each human to a place.

If doomed to roll in dust, we'll roll in dust;

we'll sit on high when destined for high seats.

Does Heaven ever favor anyone,

bestowing both rare talent and good luck?

In talent take no overweening pride,

for talent and disaster form a pair.

Our karma we must carry as our lot—

let's stop decrying Heaven's whims and quirks.

Inside ourselves there lies the root of good:

the heart outweighs all talents on this earth."[1]

---

[1] Nguyen Du, _The Tale of Kieu_, translated and annotated by Huynh Sanh Thong, Yale University Press, copyright 1983. Lines 3241-3252.

SPICY FISH SAUCE

NUOC (LIQUID) CHAM (DIPPING)

¼ cup sugar

¼ cup Vietnamese fish sauce (nuoc
mam)

¾ cup boiling water

¼ cup fresh lime or lemon juice,
including pulp

1 tbsp. sweet chili sauce

1 tbsp. sriracha chili garlic sauce

4 small or 2 large garlic cloves,
crushed

Optional garnish:

shredded carrot and/or shredded
radish (daikon)

SERVES 6   MAKES ABOUT 1 ½ CUPS

1. Combine the sugar, fish sauce and boiling water in a bowl.
Allow to cool.

2. Add lime (or lemon) juice, sweet chili sauce, chili garlic sauce
and chopped garlic. Mix thoroughly.

Nuoc Cham is served with almost all Vietnamese dishes and is
used to add flavor to salads and main courses. Without the carrot
added, it can be stored for 2-3 weeks in a covered container in the
refrigerator and added to, as needed.

PEANUT DIPPING SAUCE

NUOC (LIQUID) SOT (THICK) HAT LAC

1 tbsp. toasted sesame oil

2 cloves garlic, minced

1 tsp. chili paste

½ cup chicken broth or water

½ tsp. sugar

¼ cup crunchy peanut butter

¼ cup hoisin sauce

1 fresh red chili pepper, seeded and
    thinly sliced (optional)

3 stalks scallions, washed, trimmed
    and chopped fine

¼ cup coconut milk

Garnish:

¼ cup ground, roasted peanuts

sliced fresh, small chili pepper

SERVES 4-6   MAKES ABOUT 1 CUP

1. Grind the roasted peanuts in a food processor or grinder and set aside.

2. Heat the oil in a small saucepan. When the oil is hot, add garlic, chopped scallions and chili paste. Fry until the garlic turns golden, about ½ minute.

3. Add chicken broth or water, sugar, peanut butter and hoisin sauce and stir to dissolve the peanut butter. Bring to a boil and then reduce the heat to simmer for 3 minutes. Add coconut milk. Cool to room temperature and pour into a serving bowl or individual dipping bowls.

4. Garnish with ground, roasted peanuts and sliced fresh chili pepper.

Serve with **goi cuon (fresh spring rolls; p.2)** or **meatless cha gio (Vietnamese spring rolls; p.6).**

SWEET DIPPING SAUCE

NUOC (LIQUID) SOT (THICK) NGOT (SWEET)

8 oz. can of fruit cocktail in heavy
    syrup
1 tbsp. honey
1 tbsp. brown sugar
3 tbsp. rice vinegar
1 tbsp. soy sauce
1 tbsp. fish sauce
1 tbsp. corn starch
2 tbsp. water

SERVES 4-6   MAKES ABOUT 1 ½ CUPS

1. Grind the fruit cocktail and syrup in a blender or food processor.

2. Put the fruit and syrup in a saucepan with ½ cup of water, soy sauce, fish sauce, honey, sugar and vinegar. Bring to a boil.

3. Mix 2 tbsp. cornstarch with 2 tbsp. of water and blend thoroughly. Add cornstarch mixture to the fruit mixture and stir to thicken.

4. Cool to room temperature.

Wontons (p.12) and **eggrolls (p.10)** can be served with this sweet sauce or with a commercially prepared duck sauce.

PEANUT CURRY SAUCE

NUOC CHAM (DIPPING SAUCE) DAU PHON (PEANUT)

1 tbsp. cooking oil

1 tbsp. scallion, chopped

½ tsp. curry powder

1-2 tbsp. ground pork (optional)

½ cup peanut butter (or more)

½ cup chicken stock or bouillon
    (or water)

¼-½ cup coconut milk

½ tbsp. soy sauce

½ tbsp. fish sauce

SERVES 4-6   MAKES ABOUT 1 ½ CUPS

1. Put oil in a small saucepan, heat and add scallions to sauté.

2. Add the curry powder to the scallions, stir and then add the pork.

3. Add peanut butter, chicken stock, coconut milk, soy sauce and fish sauce.* Bring the mixture to a boil and stir to mix thoroughly.

To serve: place in a bowl or spread on top of each chicken cutlet.

Serve as a garnish for **barbecued chicken breast (p.56)** or as a dip with **sliced, fresh vegetables**.

* For a vegetarian sauce, use water instead of chicken stock, omit the ground pork and increase the coconut milk to 1 cup.

SOY/SESAME DIPPING SAUCE

NUOC TUONG TAU (CHINESE) CHAM (DIPPING)

1 tbsp. sesame seed oil

¼ cup sugar

¼ cup soy sauce

¾ cup boiling water

¼ fresh lime juice

1 tbsp. sweet chili sauce

1 tbsp. sriracha chili garlic sauce

2 large or 4 small garlic cloves,
    crushed and chopped fine

SERVES 4–6   MAKES ABOUT 1 ¼ CUPS

1. Combine sugar, soy sauce and boiling water in a bowl. Allow to cool.

2. Add lime juice, sweet chili sauce, chili garlic sauce and chopped garlic. Mix thoroughly.

Makes about 1 ¼ cups sauce, which can be stored for 2-3 weeks in a covered container in the refrigerator.

Because this recipe does not include fish sauce, it is a good dipping sauce for non-meat eaters.

SCALLION OIL

DAU (OIL) HANH (SCALLION) LA (LEAF)

4 tbsp. cooking oil (or sesame oil
  for added flavor)
4-5 scallions, minced (about 1 cup)
1 package rice noodles

SERVES 3-4 AS SIDE DISH   MAKES ⅓ CUP

1. Put the oil in a small saucepan and heat to very hot. Add the minced scallions and stir them quickly in the very hot oil until they wilt.

2. Bring a large pot of water to a boil. Add rice noodles. Cook and occasionally stir to keep them from sticking together for two minutes or until softened. Drain the noodles, put them in a bowl and pour over the hot scallion oil, which will give the noodles some flavor and prevent them from sticking together.

STIR FRY SAUCE

*(for **CHICKEN BANH HOI** and **CHICKEN BOK CHOY with EGG NOODLES**)*

NUOC (LIQUID) SAO (STIR FRY)

2 tbsp. fresh ginger root, peeled

6-7 cloves fresh garlic, peeled

1 ½ tbsp. brown sugar

1 tsp. ground black pepper

1/3 cup soy sauce

1/3 cup fish sauce

2 tbsp. hoisin sauce

1 tbsp. (or less) spicy chili garlic
    sauce

2 tbsp. rice vinegar

2 tbsp. toasted sesame oil

MAKES 1 CUP

1. In a blender or food processor, grind the ginger root, garlic, brown sugar and black pepper together.

2. Add the rest of the ingredients and grind again for 30 seconds.

Makes about 1 cup and can be stored in a covered jar in the refrigerator for 3 weeks.

Soups

Many of the soups in Vietnam combine meats, vegetables and noodles for a hearty, one dish meal. **Pho** is probably the most famous and popular soup found throughout Vietnam in small shops and market stalls. In Saigon, Pasteur Street is filled with pho shops, and many restaurants in the United States call this soup Pasteur Pho. Mien ga or chicken and bean thread soup is another of the popular and traditional Vietnamese soups.

The most flavorful and scented soups often use a stock made with lemon grass and ginger, but the Vietnamese also serve curried soups with the rich flavor of the curry seasonings combined with coconut milk.

Soup is eaten for breakfast and as a snack throughout the day as well as served with the main meal at noon and with the lighter evening supper. Many of these soups are served with crusty French bread. Although French bread is not always available in the countryside, French bakeries are common in Saigon and a reminder of the hundred years of French colonial rule.

A soup vendor serving Bun Ga.

SCENTED BEEF BROTH

PHO (FUH)

Stock:
3 lb. beef bones with some meat
   on them
12 cups water
1 tbsp. salt
2 small or 1 large onion
2 stalks lemon grass, crushed and
   chopped into 2" lengths
2-3" piece of ginger root, crushed
10-12 star anise
½ tsp. freshly ground black pepper
4 tbsp. fish sauce

Soup:
1 lb. sirloin, round or lean beef
1 lb. flat rice noodles (banh pho),
   soaked in hot water and drained
   or 1 package of fresh, flat, rice
   noodles
14 cups water
1 tsp. salt

Garnish:
1 onion, sliced in paper thin slices
   (optional)
2 stalks scallion
chopped cilantro

Vegetable platter:
1 lb. bean sprouts
1 bunch basil
1 bunch cilantro
1 hot pepper, cut into thin slices
   (optional)
1 lime, cut into 8 pieces

Flavoring sauces:
red chili sauce
hoisin sauce
fish sauce

BEEF, TRADTIONAL   SERVES 6-8

To make the stock:

1. Put the beef bones in a large pot with 14 cups of water and 1 tbsp. salt. Cut the onion in quarters and add to the pot. Smash the lemon grass with the side of a knife and cut it into 2" lengths. Smash the ginger root with the side of a knife. Add the lemon grass, ginger and the star anise to the pot and turn heat to high.

2. Bring the soup to a boil and skim off the foam with a large spoon, so that the liquid remains clear. Turn the heat down, cover the pot and simmer for 1 ½ to 2 hours. Remove from heat. Makes 8-10 cups of broth.

3. Strain the stock (for a really clear broth, strain the stock through cheese cloth); throw away the bones and flavorings; rinse out the pot and pour the clear broth back in. Add the ½ tsp. ground black pepper.

4. For an even clearer broth, store the stock in the refrigerator overnight and scrape off the fat the next morning. The stock can be portioned and frozen in Ziploc bags and stored indefinitely.

To make the soup:

1. Put the beef in the freezer long enough to stiffen and then slice the beef into thin shreds, about 1-2" long.

2. Wash the greens for the vegetable platter and arrange them on a serving dish. Slice the hot pepper into very thin slices and arrange the slices on the dish. Cut the lime into 8 pieces and add those to the dish.

3. Pour the chili sauce, hoisin sauce and fish sauce into small serving bowls.

4. Bring 10 cups of water and 1 tsp. salt to a boil in a large pot. Add the rice noodles and cook for 8 minutes. Drain the noodles; cut them into 3" lengths and divide them into 6-8, large soup bowls. (For fresh noodles, bring 10 cups of water to a boil, submerge the noodles in the boiling water and then drain.)

5. Garnish: Slice the onion into very thin slices. Cut the scallions into 2" lengths, and loosely chop the cilantro leaves. Arrange with the other ingredients on the vegetable platter.

To serve:

1. Bring the soup stock back to a boil. Add the 4 tbsp. fish sauce. Put some uncooked beef slices on top of the cooked noodles in the individual soup bowls. Ladle the stock into the bowls to cover the noodles and beef so that the stock cooks the beef.

2. Each person can add vegetables, garnishes and sauces to taste.

Pho is one of the most well-known, popular and traditional Vietnamese dishes. It is frequently sold by street vendors throughout Vietnam and eaten for breakfast, lunch or dinner. Except for making the stock, this soup is quick and easy to prepare. The scent of the cooking broth, with its anise, lemon grass, ginger, and onion will fill the house, and in Vietnam, Pho perfume fills the city streets, particularly Pasteur Street, one of the most famous streets in Saigon. In Vietnamese-American restaurants, the menu often lists this soup as "Pasteur Pho."

One of Mai's favorite memories of Vietnam was her Godmother preparing Pho over a small charcoal stove in her bedroom just before Mai left with her husband and new baby for the USA.

Pho, with its fresh vegetable platter, sauces, beef cooked to order, and aromatic clear broth, embodies all the basic elements of Vietnamese cuisine and hospitality.

CHICKEN & BEAN THREAD SOUP

MIEN (CROWN) GA (CHICKEN)

3 lb. whole chicken or 2 chicken legs
and 2 breasts

1" slice ginger root, unpeeled

1 onion, quartered

2 chicken bouillon cubes

3, 1.8 oz. packets of bean thread

3 tbsp. fish sauce

½ tsp. ground black pepper

2 tbsp. (1 stalk) chopped scallion,
for garnish

4 stalks of cilantro, for garnish

CHICKEN, TRADITIONAL   SERVES 6-8

1. Wash the chicken and put it in a large pot and cover with water. Put the pot over high heat and bring to a boil. Smash the ginger with the side of a knife and add it to the chicken pot. Peel the onion and cut it in quarters. Add the onion and 2 chicken bouillon cubes to the pot. Bring to a boil and then simmer for about 45 minutes uncovered. Skim off any foam to keep the stock clear.

2. Put the bean thread in a bowl and cover with warm water to soak for about 15 minutes. Drain the bean thread and cut it into 2-3" pieces with kitchen shears or a knife. Set aside.

3. Remove the chicken from the broth and allow to cool. Bone, skin and shred the chicken.

4. Strain the chicken broth to a clear liquid and pour it back into the pot. Turn the heat to high and bring the stock to a full boil, skimming any fat that accumulates on the surface. Add the black pepper and fish sauce.

5. Add the chicken to the stock, and just before serving, add the bean thread, and turn off the heat. Garnish with chopped scallions and cilantro.

Free-range chickens and a
rooster in the courtyard.

Mai had a pet chicken, which was part of her dowry. When the chicken hatched five roosters from its first eggs, it did not take long for the roosters to begin fighting amongst themselves. Mai's mother gave the first rooster to provide the main course for the wedding dinner of a village girl too poor to buy her own chicken. The bride's family then showed their gratitude for the gift by working in Mai's family's rice fields. The rest of the roosters were sold in the city for cockfighting.

This very rich chicken soup is served by street vendors all over Vietnam and is eaten as a snack throughout the day or as the main course at mealtime.

CHICKEN & RICE NOODLE SOUP with BEAN SPROUTS

BUN (NOODLE) GA (CHICKEN)

Ingredients for stock:

3-4 lb. chicken necks and backs or a
    whole chicken

10 cups water

½ tsp. salt

1 piece fresh ginger root, about 1" thick

1 onion, cut in quarters

1 stalk lemongrass, cut in 2" pieces

½ cup fish sauce

½ tsp. freshly ground pepper

For the soup:

8 cups water

½ tsp. salt

1 (8 oz.) package rice stick noodles

1 bunch scallions, chopped

1 sprig, chopped fresh cilantro

1 ½ cups fresh bean sprouts

1-2 lemons, quartered

CHICKEN   SERVES 6-8

1. If using a whole chicken, cut it into quarters. Bring 10 cups of water and ½ tsp. salt to a boil in a large pot. Add the chicken pieces and bring back to a boil. Skim the foam off the top. Add ginger root, onion and lemongrass. Simmer for 45 minutes, skimming the fat and foam off the top. Remove the chicken, allow it to cool and then remove the skin and bones and shred the chicken. Set aside. Strain the stock through cheesecloth or a strainer. Makes about 10 cups of stock.

2. For the noodles: Bring 8 cups of water and ½ tsp. salt to a boil in a large pot. Add the rice noodles and cook over medium heat for 4-5 minutes. Drain the noodles in a colander. Set aside.

3. Bring the chicken stock back to a boil. Add the fish sauce and black pepper.

4. Put 1 cup rice noodles and ½ cup cooked chicken in individual soup bowls. Ladle stock over the noodles and chicken. Garnish with cilantro and scallions and serve with a platter of bean sprouts and lemon wedges to be added to taste.

SOUR & SPICY SHRIMP SOUP

CANH (SOUP) CAY (SPICY) CHUA (SOUR) NGOT (SWEET)

2 cups taro root (2 small corms)

2 large tomatoes

2 cups fresh pineapple

1 sweet red pepper

2 cups okra (about 20)

1 lb. uncooked shrimp, peeled and
    deveined

8 cups chicken stock

2 tbsp. instant hot and sour paste
    (available in Asian markets)

2 tbsp. tamarind sweet and sour
    soup base powder

½ tbsp. sugar

¼ cup fish sauce

1 lb. bean sprouts.

Garnish with:

2 Thai hot peppers, chopped fine
    (optional)

2 scallions, cleaned, trimmed and
    chopped

10 stalks of Asian mint, chopped
    (optional)

10 stalks of cilantro, trimmed and
    chopped

SHRIMP   SERVES 4-6

1. Peel off the outer layer of the taro root and mince. Chop the tomatoes, pineapple and red pepper into bite-sized pieces. Trim off the ends of the okra and slice in half, lengthwise. Rinse, peel and devein the shrimp.

2. Bring the 8 cups of chicken stock to a boil in a large soup pot. Add the instant hot and sour paste, the tamarind sweet and sour soup base powder and the sugar. When the stock returns to a boil, add the taro, tomatoes, pineapple, red pepper and okra. Bring back to a boil and skim off the foam. Add the shrimp and fish sauce and bring back to a boil. Then stir in the bean sprouts. Garnish with chopped scallions and mint or cilantro. Sprinkle with Thai hot pepper to taste (optional).

Serve as a first course or as a main dish with **steamed rice (p.016)**, **French bread** or **salad.**

CHICKEN & RICE SOUP

CHAO GA (CHICKEN)

½ cup uncooked rice

3 cubes chicken bouillon

3 lb. whole chicken or 2 legs and 2
    breasts

1" slice ginger root, unpeeled

1 medium onion

1 tsp. salt

¼ cup fish sauce

dash, fresh ground black pepper

2 stalks scallion, chopped

2 stalks cilantro, chopped

CHICKEN   SERVES 4-6

1. Put ½ cup rice, 1 bouillon cube and 1 cup water in a pan over high heat and bring to a boil. Turn the heat down, cover the pot and simmer until the rice is cooked (about 20 minutes) to make 2-3 cups cooked rice.

2. Put whole chicken or chicken parts in a large soup pot and cover with 5-6 cups of water. Smash the ginger slice with the side of a large knife and add to the chicken and water. Cut the onion into quarters and add to the pot. Bring the pot to a rolling boil and skim the fat and foam from the surface with a large spoon. Cover the pot and lower the heat to a simmer and cook for another 30-40 minutes until chicken is cooked through.

3. Remove the chicken from the pot and let cool. Skim the fat from the broth and strain the broth to a clear liquid. Add 2 bouillon cubes to the broth.

4. Skin, bone and shred the chicken and return the chicken meat to the broth along with the cooked rice. Bring the broth to a full boil. Add the fish sauce and black pepper. Stir and remove from the heat and garnish with chopped scallions and chopped cilantro.

This is a rich, chicken soup and a favorite with Mai's children on a cold, rainy day or when they feel under the weather.

Plucking and carefully washing
a freshly-killed chicken.

When Mai was growing up in Vietnam, the government regulated all the food in the country. During the day, the average Vietnamese family ate rice, sweet potatoes, bananas or whatever they could grow in their own gardens, but chickens, fresh crops and eggs were frequently appropriated by the authorities.

Whenever Mai serves chicken soup, she thinks of her mother and family, awakened at 2 AM and drinking soup around the light of a single coconut lamp so they could escape detection by the authorities.

After they finished eating, Mai's mother would send her children back to their mats to sleep and go out into the courtyard to bury the chicken fat and bones.

EGG & RICE SOUP

GONZE (CHINESE CHICKEN RICE SOUP)

¼ cup sweet rice (if available)

½ cup white rice (or ¾ cup white
    rice if you have no sweet rice)

½ tsp. salt

6 cups water

3 eggs

2 scallions, washed, trimmed and
    chopped fine

¼ tsp. fresh ground black pepper

1 ½ tbsp. fish sauce

Garnish:

2 stalks cilantro

1 scallion, washed, trimmed and
    chopped fine

EGG   SERVES 4

1. Rinse the two rices, drain and add 6 cups of water and ½ tsp. salt. Bring the water to a boil and then turn down the heat and let simmer for 17-20 minutes. The rice will only absorb some of the water. The rest of the water is the soup base.

2. Break the 3 eggs into a bowl. Add the freshly ground black pepper, fish sauce and chopped green onions and beat together.

3. Bring the rice soup back to a boil and slowly stir in the egg mixture. Allow the egg mixture to set (about 1 minute) and then serve the soup hot, garnished with cilantro and scallions.

All of Mai's children like to come home for Christmas and particularly be together for meals. In preparation for these gatherings, Mai usually stocks up on fresh vegetables, fruit, and meat and spends days cooking. One Christmas, Mai's older son came home from California with a new girlfriend, who was a vegetarian. Although Mai's refrigerator was full of fresh vegetables and fruit, her prepared foods in the freezer were meat dishes. For that first night, Mai did not want her son's girlfriend to go hungry, so she made her this simple egg and rice soup, which the girlfriend apparently loved, because she eventually agreed to marry Mai's son.

WINTER/FUZZY MELON SOUP

CANH (SOUP) DUA LONG (FUZZY MELON)

½ lb. shrimp, peeled and
    de-veined

5 scallions

1 tsp. freshly ground black pepper

4 tbsp. fish sauce

6 cups chicken broth

½ cup water

1 fuzzy (winter) melon, about 1 lb.
    (or substitute 1 lb. zucchini)

3 scallions, trimmed and chopped

2 stalks cilantro, cleaned and
    chopped

SHRIMP   SERVES 6-8

1. Peel the fuzzy skin off the melon. Rinse the melon and cut it into quarters, lengthwise, and then cut it again into thin slices.

2. Peel and devein the shrimp and set aside.

3. Wash the 5 scallions and cut into 1" lengths.

4. Put the scallions, shrimp and black pepper into the bowl of a food processor and grind to a paste with the metal blade. Add 4 tbsp. of fish sauce to the shrimp mixture and grind again. Turn the shrimp mixture out into a bowl. Add ½ cup water and stir to mix with a fork or chopsticks.

5. Put the 6 cups of chicken broth into a medium saucepan over high heat, and bring to a boil. Add shrimp mixture and boil for one minute, stirring to break into pieces. Skim off the foam from the surface of the soup but not the shrimp pieces. Add the fuzzy melon and cook for 5 more minutes. Garnish with chopped scallions and cilantro.

This soup can be served hot, cold or at room temperature. Serve with **steamed rice (p.106)**.

BITTER MELON SOUP

U GUA (BITTER MELON) DONG (STUFFED) THIT (MEAT)

4 bitter melons

½ lb. ground pork

¼ lb. shrimp, peeled and deveined

3 scallions

½ cup bean thread

¼ tsp. freshly ground black pepper

2 tbsp. fish sauce

5 cups chicken stock (3 cans)

4 scallions

PORK & SHRIMP, TRADITIONAL   SERVES 8

1. Slit the bitter melon down its length on one side and scoop out the seeds, leaving the melon whole but hollow for filling.

2. Soak the bean thread in a bowl of warm water for 10-15 minutes. Drain and chop the bean thread into small pieces.

3. Grind the shrimp in the bowl of a food processor. Add the scallions and grind again. Add the ground pork and bean thread and grind again to mix thoroughly. Add the black pepper and fish sauce and mix together.

4. Fill the cavity of the hollowed out bitter melon with the pork and shrimp mixture.

5. Pour the chicken stock into a large pot over high heat and bring to a boil.

6. Cut four, long green leaves from the scallions and dip each of the leaves into the boiling stock to make the leaves wilted and pliable. Wrap each scallion leaf around a bitter melon and tie so that the melon will stay closed during cooking. (If the scallion leaves are too short, slit them in half and tie the two pieces together before wrapping around the melon.) Place the stuffed melons in the boiling chicken stock and simmer for 1 hour.

To serve, cut each melon in half and put in individual soup bowls. Ladle the chicken stock over the melon halves. Garnish with chopped scallions. Serve with **steamed rice (p.106).**

Although the broth of this soup is very bitter and medicinal tasting, it is very high in vitamins and considered a restorative in the Vietnam countryside. Mai's Godmother would always have this soup ready to serve to her husband at the end of his late night card games.

CURRIED CHICKEN, MUSHROOM, & COCONUT MILK SOUP

CANH (SOUP) GA (CHICKEN) NUOC (LIQUID) DUA (COCONUT)

1 whole chicken breast, split, boned,
   skinned and cut into 1" cubes

2 tbsp. canola or corn oil

6 cups chicken stock

1 (15 oz.) can straw mushrooms,
   drained

1 cup coconut milk

1 tbsp. canola or corn oil

2 tbsp. fish sauce

For marinade:

1 large stalk lemon grass

1 large clove garlic, peeled

1 shallot, peeled

2 ½ tsp. curry powder

½ tbsp. sugar

1 tsp. salt

Garnish:

5 stalks cilantro, cleaned and
   chopped

½ cup ground peanuts

1 lime, cut into wedges.

Optional: white rice or French bread

CURRIED   SERVES 6-8

1. To make the marinade, cut off the bottom inch of the lemon grass, peel off the tough outer layer, smash with a meat mallet or the side of a knife and chop into thin slices. In a mortar and pestle or food processer, add the lemon grass, garlic, shallot, curry powder, sugar and salt and grind to a paste.

2. In a medium saucepan, add the 2 tbsp. of canola or corn oil and turn the heat to high. Add the marinade and sauté for 1 minute. Add the cubed chicken and cook, stirring until the chicken is lightly browned (3 minutes). Add the chicken stock and bring to a boil. Add the straw mushrooms and cook for another minute. Add the fish sauce and then the coconut milk. Stir and heat through but do not boil.

3. Garnish with chopped cilantro, ground peanuts and lime wedges.

Serve soup hot with **French bread** or **white rice.**

This is Mai's variation on a favorite Thai soup. She has reduced the oil and coconut milk in the recipe to make it a lighter, lower fat dish.

SPINACH SOUP with PORK & SHRIMP

RAU BA-LANG (SPINACH) VA (WITH) TOM (SHRIMP), THIT HEO (PORK MEAT)

½ lb. pork tenderloin (or ground pork)

8 medium shrimp (¼ lb.), peeled and deveined

1 stalk scallion, chopped

1" piece, fresh ginger root, peeled and minced

2 chicken bouillon cubes (or chicken stock)

4 tbsp. fish sauce

1 tsp. black pepper

6 cups water

1 lb. (1 ½ packages) fresh spinach (or substitute mustard greens, escarole, bok choy or other greens)

2 small packets (1.8 oz. each) bean thread (Chinese vermicelli)

5 stalks cilantro, cleaned and chopped

PORK & SHRIMP   SERVES 4

1. Cut the pork into cubes. Peel and devein the shrimp. Wash and chop the scallion and mince the ginger root.

2. In a food processor, add the cubed pork and grind (or use ground pork), then add the shrimp, the scallion and ginger. Add fish sauce and black pepper and mix thoroughly.

3. Cover the bean thread with hot water and let soak. Drain and set aside.

4. In a large sauce pan, add 6 cups of water and bring to a boil. Using chopsticks or a teaspoon, add 1 tsp. of the pork-shrimp mixture at a time to the boiling water until all the mixture has been added. (Or form the pork-shrimp mixture into 1" meatballs and drop them into the boiling water.) Skim off the foam. The mixture is cooked when it floats to the top. Add the spinach and stir until the spinach wilts. Add the softened bean thread and garnish with chopped cilantro.

Serve hot or cold.

Mai adding the pork and shrimp
meatballs to the soup.

Mai's mother was both proud and generous, and when she returned home one evening to find that the maid was feeding her children rice and spinach soup without any meat, she promptly sat down and wept. She did not want her tenants or her maid to think that she could not provide for her family. Only the poorest Vietnamese would serve spinach and rice soup without meat, and on special holidays like Tet, the tenant farmers would serve the soup with a "square pig": the head, feet and tail without the body. This soup, with its tasty pork and shrimp meatballs, can be served as a main course that would make even Mai's mother proud.

SWEET POTATO SOUP

CANH (SOUP) KOAI LANG (POTATO) NGOT (SWEET)

4 medium yams or sweet potatoes
(3 lb.)

2 tbsp. cooking oil

3 cloves garlic

1 tbsp. curry powder

2 (13 oz.) cans chicken stock (or 3
cups of fresh chicken stock or
3 cups water for a vegetarian
soup)

½ cup unsalted, roasted peanuts

2 tbsp. fish sauce (4 tbsp. if you use
water instead of stock)

1 tsp. sugar

1 cup coconut milk

2 scallions, chopped

CURRIED   SERVES 6

1. Peel the sweet potatoes and cut them into large cubes (about 1 ½").

2. Smash the garlic with the side of a large knife and mince.

3. Put the oil in a large pot over high heat. Add the garlic and brown. Add the curry powder and the chicken stock to the pot. Add the sweet potato cubes and ½ cup of unsalted peanuts. Bring the pot to a boil, cover and cook for ½ hour until the potatoes are softened but not mushy. Add the sugar, fish sauce and coconut milk to the pot and stir to mix. (If the coconut milk has separated in the can, stir before adding to the soup. Leftover coconut milk can be stored in a plastic freezer bag and frozen.) Garnish with the chopped scallions.

This is a very hearty and filling soup. It is a wonderful vegetarian meal cooked with water instead of chicken stock. Serve with **crusty French bread.**

Woman carrying bundles of kindling in her right hand
and sweet potato plants in her left hand.

In the small villages, the Vietnamese cook whatever they can grow. Although pork and chicken are available, they are expensive and used sparingly. Beef was available primarily when a work animal was old or had been shot accidentally in one of the many skirmishes that characterized the war years in the countryside.

When sweet potatoes are boiled, sliced and then dried and stored in large, clay pots or in baskets hung from the rafters, they are a favorite Vietnamese snack.

One evening Mai's family was visited by a group of several young people from the village. While the others sat talking, Mai slipped outside to dip some sweet potato slices into a big pot of brown sugar that was kept in the courtyard. Bending over the pot, Mai saw one of the young men come out to join her. With their heads bent over the sugar pot, he whispered that two of the group inside were Viet Cong and had come to take her away. Without going back inside, Mai left the courtyard and ran away. She would not see her home or village again for more than 30 years.

Main Dishes

Many of the main dishes served in Vietnam are stir fries, but the marinade for the meat is much lighter than the marinades used in Chinese cooking. Fish sauce, garlic and ginger are the staples for the marinades, with variations including lemon grass, soy sauce, and chili peppers. Mai rarely uses any oil in a marinade and uses very little in her cooking. She keeps the food from sticking to the pan or wok by heating the oil very hot before adding the meats, and she rarely thickens her sauces with cornstarch.

Most of these recipes are very low in fat, and although several have many ingredients, preparation time is reasonable if you use a food processor. Many ingredients are served fresh as a salad platter and only require rinsing and slicing or chopping.

Although chopsticks are always offered, many of these dishes are more easily eaten with fingers.

The dishes at the end of this section are more complicated, and although they are still home-style cooking, they are often served at a holiday banquet or special occasion.

When Mai lived in Saigon, she would occasionally take day trips to Chau Doc, southwest of the city, or Tay Ninh, the capital city of the Cao Dai religion. Day trips were somewhat risky, because the Viet Cong controlled many of the villages and hamlets outside of Saigon, and Mai's visits had less to do with religion than the adventure of the excursion and the consultation with one of the numerous fortune tellers in the region.

Fortune tellers, shaman, and wisemen are consulted in Vietnam whenever a well needs digging, a new house needs proper orientation, an auspicious day and time for a marriage needs to be chosen, or when a journey or a new venture is about to begin. Fortunes are gained or lost with the toss of the jah sticks, the dealing of the cards, the curling smoke of the incense and, most often, with meditation and the visitation of spirits.

The spirits of the ancestors are reincarnated in animals or people, linger in the roof beams, at the grave sites, and within the cabinets where the most prized possessions are stored, and they reside comfortably alongside the teachings of Buddha, Confucius, and Christ. It is these spirits that are continuously consulted, appeased, nourished and honored to give the Vietnamese some sense of control over their fates.

STIR-FRY CHICKEN WRAPPED in LETTUCE

GA (CHICKEN) BANH (PURSE) HOI (ASK FOR)

For the chicken: (or substitute beef, shrimp or tofu)

Stir fry sauce (p.27)

1 lb. chicken breast, boned, skinned and sliced thin

1 medium onion, sliced in thin wedges

3 scallions, washed, trimmed and cut in 1" pieces

½ cup ground peanuts

2 tbsp. canola or corn oil

For the noodles:

6 cups water

½ package banh hoi (fine rice) noodles

½ tsp. salt

4 scallions, minced

4 tbsp. cooking oil

For the fresh salad:

1 green plantain (or banana), sliced thin

1 small cucumber, peeled, seeded, cut in half and sliced thin

1 small, green mango, sliced in thin shreds (if available)

1 starfruit, sliced thin (if available)

1 cup bean sprouts

6 leaves of romaine or leaf lettuce

4 stalks fresh mint

4 stalks fresh basil

Nuoc cham (spicy fish sauce; p.21)

FINGERFOOD   SERVES 4-6

1. Put the boned and skinned chicken breast in the freezer to make it easier to slice.

2. Heat the cooking oil in a wok or frying pan. Add the chicken and onion and stir with chopsticks or a wooden spoon for 1-2 minutes. Carefully (so it does not spit), pour the stir-fry sauce around the brim of the pan and then stir in with the chicken and onion. Add the scallions; transfer the chicken mixture to a serving platter and garnish with ground peanuts.

3. Put 6 cups of water and ½ tsp. salt in a large pot and bring to a boil. Add the banh hoi noodles and bring back to a boil. Drain the noodles in a colander and rinse with cold water. Mix in the scallions and oil and put on a serving platter.

4. Wash and dry the salad greens, bean sprouts, mint and basil and spread them on the platter with the rice noodles.

5. Peel the plantain and cut into paper-thin slices, on a diagonal. Peel, seed and cut the cucumber into thin slices on the diagonal. (If you are using a medium to large cucumber, cut the slices in half or into matchsticks.) If available, peel the skin off the mango and cut the pulp into thin shreds. Slice the starfruit into paper thin slices and arrange all the fruits on the serving platter.

6. Using a lettuce leaf as a wrapper, fill the leaf with a selection of greens, fruits, herbs, noodles and the chicken mixture and roll up the leaf. Dip the filled lettuce leaf in the nuoc cham and enjoy!

Chicken banh hoi is a salad platter that combines fruits as well as vegetables with a stir-fried or grilled meat. Mangos, starfruit and other tropical fruits are added in season, but the dish always includes rice noodles, cucumbers and plantains. The plantain, which is similar in shape to a banana, is not as sweet or soft and, therefore, will not fall apart in serving. The **nuoc cham** or spicy fish sauce is sometimes sweetened for this recipe to complement the fruit.

Mai's mother told her children that the crow was turned ugly by magic because it kept stealing from the other birds, and on the outskirts of Mai's village, there was a very ugly young man who lived with his mother and did very little work. When his mother died, he continued to live alone and did not seek work, and the villagers eventually noticed that someone was leaving an empty rice noodle basket instead of refilling it with fresh rice and some of the chickens foraging in the courtyards were disappearing.

When Mai and her cousin Diem discovered one of their chickens missing, they found strange footprints in the corner of their courtyard, and the two young girls decided to follow the footprints and ended up at the home of the ugly and lazy young man, who was busy plucking the last feathers from the stolen chicken. Thrilled at solving the mystery of the disappearing rice noodles and chicken, the two girls told the ugly man that they would go to the oldest man in the village and tell him who was stealing the food. Since the oldest man served as both judge and jury for Thong An Ninh, the ugly man could expect to be punished and sent away or forced to work for the families from whom he had stolen.

The ugly, young man promised never to steal again and went to work in the rice fields for food. The chickens stopped disappearing, and the man was never punished, although he continued to live alone and remained very ugly.

FRIED RICE STICK CHICKEN SALAD

BUN (NOODLE) CHIEN (FRY) GON (CRISPY) TRONG (MIXED) GA (CHICKEN)

2 whole chicken breasts, boned and
    skinned

2" piece of ginger root

½ cup red cabbage, shredded

1 cup carrot, shredded

½ cup bean sprouts

½ cup basil leaves

½ cup cilantro leaves

4 scallions

1 cup lettuce, shredded

2 ½ cups cooking oil

¾ lb. medium rice stick noodles

2 tbsp. fish sauce

2 tbsp. soy sauce

¼ tsp. freshly ground black pepper

2 cloves garlic, minced

1 tbsp. cooking oil

1 cup salted peanuts, ground

2 cups, **nuoc cham (spicy fish
    sauce; p.21)**

SERVES 4-6

1. Cut the chicken into shreds. Peel the ginger piece and slice in very thin matchstick slivers. Add the ginger, 2 tbsp. soy sauce, 2 tbsp. fish sauce, and ¼ tsp. black pepper to the chicken shreds and let marinate.

2. Wash and shred the lettuce and put in a large bowl. Shred the cabbage into very fine pieces and then shred the carrots and add the cabbage and carrots to the lettuce. (To shred, use a shredder, a large holed grater or a food processor.) Cut the scallions into 2" lengths and add to the salad bowl. Separate the basil and cilantro leaves from their stems and put them in the salad. Wash and add the bean sprouts. Set the salad aside.

3. Heat the 2 ½ cups of cooking oil in a wok until it is very hot. (To test the oil, drop in a rice noodle. It should curl, whiten and puff up immediately if the oil is hot enough.) Separating the rice noodles into small bunches (about 9 bunches for ¾ pound), pick up one bunch of noodles with tongs or chopsticks and immerse the noodles in the hot oil. Push the noodles down into the oil for about 20-30 seconds until they puff up, curl and whiten, and then turn the noodles over and push them down again for another 20-30 seconds. The noodles should not brown. Remove the noodles from the oil and allow to drain on a paper towel.

4. Remove the cooking oil from the wok and wipe the bottom of the wok clean. Add 1 tbsp. cooking oil to the wok and heat it until it is very hot. Smash the garlic with the side of the knife and mince it and add it to the wok. Stir and then add the chicken mixture and cook, stirring, until the chicken is cooked through (about 5-10 minutes).

5. In a very large salad bowl or platter, place the fried, rice noodles. Place the fresh salad ingredients over the noodles and then add the chicken mixture. Sprinkle the top with the ground peanuts and mix everything together. Put the portions on plates individually and spoon the nuoc cham over the salad like salad dressing.

This salad can be made ahead but should be assembled just before serving. To keep the rice noodles from becoming limp after frying, cover them or seal them in plastic bags.

For a variation, you can substitute 1 ½ lb. peeled shrimp for the chicken.

In Thong An Ninh, the monsoon season lasts from August through October, but during the hot and still days of summer, the Vietnamese in the countryside eat most of their meals outdoors under the roof overhangs or fruit trees. During the particularly hot days, Mai filled a shallow, cement basin in the courtyard with water and sat in it while eating. Before the noon meal and at the end of the work day, everyone would shower by pouring buckets of well water over themselves and their work clothes, and after the meal, they would nap through the hottest part of the day before returning to the fields.

This salad is a wonderful and particularly light main dish for a hot, summer day. It has an interesting combination of textures and flavors, with a strong taste of ginger in the chicken for balance. The noodles are crispy, but because the rice does not absorb the oil, this dish is far lighter than it would be with fried egg noodles. The nuoc cham also contains no oil, making this a good, low fat, diet dish.

CHICKEN & CABBAGE SALAD

BAP CAI (CABBAGE) GA (CHICKEN)

3 lb. whole chicken or 1 whole chicken breast

1" piece ginger, sliced in half and smashed with the handle of a knife

1 small head of cabbage (1-1¼ lb.), shredded

2 large carrots, shredded

1 cup unsalted, roasted peanuts, ground

½ bunch basil, washed (about 1 cup)

½ cup scallions, green part only, chopped

¼-½ tsp. freshly ground black pepper

Ingredients for dressing (makes ¾ cup):

1-2 lemons, fresh squeezed for the juice (¼ cup juice)

2-4 cloves garlic, smashed

1-2 tsp. sweet chili sauce (or substitute ¼ tsp. crushed, red pepper)

¼ cup sugar

¼ cup fish sauce

2-3 tbsp. sesame oil (optional)

Garnish:

red cabbage leaves, shredded

SERVES 8-10

1. Put the chicken in a large pot with 4 cups of water and the ginger. Bring to a boil. Skim off any scum layer on top of water. Cover the pot and turn the heat to medium low and simmer for 20-25 minutes. Turn off the heat but leave the pot covered for another 30-35 minutes to cook chicken meat through but not overcook.

2. Shred the cabbage with a knife or food processor and put in a large bowl. Shred the carrots and mix with the cabbage in the bowl.

3. Remove the skin and bones from the chicken and break the meat into thin shreds. (Save chicken stock for soup or another recipe. Stock can be frozen for later use.)

4. Smash the garlic with the handle of the knife or grind in a mortar and then mix with sugar, lemon juice, chili sauce and fish sauce in a bowl.

5. Add the chicken, whole basil leaves and chopped scallions to the bowl of shredded cabbage and carrots. Mix together. Pour the dressing over the salad and mix again. Grind black pepper over the top. Grind the peanuts in a grinder or food processor and pour ½ cup over the salad. Mix again. Turn the salad out onto a platter and surround with shredded red cabbage leaves and top with the remaining ½ cup of ground peanuts.

This light and refreshing salad can be made ahead of time but should be assembled with the dressing only when ready to serve. Serve alone or with shrimp chips or sesame crackers (see **Asian Ingredients, p.126**).

VIETNAMESE CHICKEN SANDWICH

THIT GA (CHICKEN MEAT) BANH MI (SANDWICH)

For the meat:

1 lb. boneless, skinless chicken
    breast, sliced thin

1 ½ tbsp. soy sauce

¼ cup Italian salad dressing

Other ingredients:

4 submarine sandwich rolls or a
    baguette cut into 6" lengths

3 tbsp. olive oil

1 cup **pickled radishes and carrot
    (p.16)**

4 eggs (optional)

4 large Romaine lettuce leaves

½ cucumber, sliced thin

4 large scallions, trimmed and sliced
    in half lengthwise

8 stalks cilantro

½ cup real mayonnaise

1-2 tsp. sriracha hot sauce

SERVES 4

1. Mix the chicken, soy sauce and Italian dressing in a bowl and set aside.

2. Peel and shred 1 lb. radishes and carrots and marinate in ½ cup sugar, ¾ cup white vinegar, and 1 tsp. salt for several hours or overnight.

3. Heat 2 tbsp. of olive oil in a fry pan over medium heat. Add the chicken mixture and stir-fry for 3-5 minutes until meat is browned and cooked through. Remove the meat from the pan and set aside. In the same fry pan, add 1 tbsp. olive oil and fry the four eggs over low heat until they are cooked through. Remove the eggs from the pan and cut each one in half.

4. Slice the hoagie rolls in half and lightly toast or crisp in the heated, dry fry pan.

5. Mix together the mayonnaise and sriracha hot sauce and spread on each side of the hoagie rolls. Add the chicken, fried egg halves, scallions, sliced cucumber, pickled carrot and radishes, cilantro and lettuce.

Asian cuisine tries to balance flavors, textures and smells: sweet and either salty or spicy, smooth and crisp, cooked and raw, and the Vietnamese sandwich (Banh Mi) is famous for its spicy sauce, marinated meats and pickled vegetables, offering the perfect balance of crisp, crunchy, spicy and flavorful. Instead of chicken, pulled or sliced pork or even pate' can be substituted.

CHICKEN WITH BOK CHOY & EGG NOODLES

MI (NOODLE) XAO (STIR FRY) GA (CHICKEN) BAP CAI (CABBAGE)

Stir fry sauce (see **Sauces, p.27**)

1 lb. egg noodles (fresh or dried and the diameter of spaghetti noodles)

10 cups water

2 tsp. salt

2 whole, boneless, skinless chicken breasts (about 1 lb.) or substitute beef, shrimp or fried tofu

3 cloves garlic

2 tbsp. canola or corn oil

1 lb. bok choy (Chinese cabbage or substitute broccoli or cabbage)

2 carrots

½ lb. bean sprouts

Garnish:

½ cup ground peanuts

several sprigs of cilantro

2 scallions, chopped

SERVES 6

1. Prepare the stir-fry sauce and set aside.

2. Fill a large pot with 10 cups of water, add 2 tsp. salt and bring the water to a boil over high heat. Add the egg noodles and cook 3-4 minutes if the noodles are dried or 1-2 minutes if the noodles are fresh. Drain the noodles and rinse with cold water. Cut the noodles into 4" lengths and pour 2 ½ tbsp. of the stir-fry sauce over the noodles, mix thoroughly and set aside.

3. Chop the bok choy into 1" pieces; shred the carrots and set both aside. Rinse and drain the bean sprouts. Mince the 3 cloves of garlic.

4. Put the chicken in the freezer long enough to make it easier to cut, against the grain, into thin slices, and then separate the chicken slices into two batches. In a wok or fry pan, add 1 tbsp. of canola oil and turn heat to high. Add the garlic and stir until lightly browned before adding the first batch of chicken. Stir-fry for 1 minute and then pour 1 tbsp. of the stir-fry sauce around the edge of the pan before mixing it with the chicken and garlic, cooking 3-4 more minutes or until the chicken is cooked through. Remove the chicken and set aside.

5. Heat the fry pan again with another 1 tbsp. of canola oil and add the second batch of chicken and another 1 tbsp. of the stir-fry sauce. Cook for 3-4 minutes or until cooked through. Put both batches of chicken back in the wok or fry pan, Add the chopped bok choy and shredded carrots and stir-fry for 1 minute. Add the bean sprouts and the rest of the stir-fry sauce and stir-fry for another 2 minutes before adding the cooked noodles. Stir everything until heated through and transfer to a serving platter.

6. Garnish with ground peanuts, cilantro and chopped scallions.

This recipe can be easily doubled or tripled, although the noodles should be cooked in batches. For vegetarians, substitute chili paste or fried tofu for the chicken. Can be prepared ahead and served hot or cold.

BARBECUED CHICKEN BREAST

THIT GA (CHICKEN MEAT) NUONG (BARBECUED)

2 ½ lb. boneless chicken breasts (4 breasts), skinned, and sliced in thin cutlets

Ingredients for marinade:

¼ tsp. black pepper

2 stalks lemon grass, crushed and chopped

2" piece of unpeeled ginger root, chopped

2 cloves garlic, peeled and chopped

4 tbsp. fish sauce

3 tbsp. soy sauce

2 ½ tbsp. brown sugar

3 tbsp. olive oil

1 tbsp. Worcestershire sauce

SERVES 4

1. Put the pepper, lemon grass, ginger root, and garlic in a mortar or a food processor and grind (a mortar and pestle gives a rougher and better texture). Add brown sugar, fish sauce, soy sauce, olive oil and Worcestershire sauce and mix together. Pour the marinade over the chicken cutlets. Marinate at least 1 hour but do not marinate more than 12 hours or the chicken will lose its texture.

2. Cook the chicken on a very hot grill for 3-5 minutes on each side.

Serve with **peanut curry sauce (p.24), steamed rice (p.106)** and **marinated cucumbers (p.13).**

This barbecued chicken cutlet is light and delicious on its own but is a heartier main dish when served with the peanut curry sauce**.**

In Vietnam, cooking is done outdoors over charcoal or an open fire, as most kitchens have neither a stove nor an oven. Mai's mother cooks outside in the courtyard or on the dirt floor of a cooking shed. She makes her wood or charcoal fire on the ground between three bent over clay figures called "Kitchen Gods", which hold her clay cooking pots or wok. Two of the clay figures represent the kitchen helpers and the third is the Kitchen God himself, always distinguished by an indentation representing the belly button. One morning after an argument with her mother, Mai hit the Kitchen God with the large stick she used for stirring the fire. Although the Kitchen God did not break, Mai's mother banished Mai from the kitchen, certain that bad luck would follow this show of disrespect. Mai's mother then offered sweet rice to assuage the Kitchen God's anger and tossed two old coins onto a plate. When both coins turned up with matching heads, Mai's mother was assured that the Kitchen God was no longer angry, and she and Mai could continue preparing the meal.

Heaven was once nearer the earth, but when human thieves stole its light, the gods moved heaven further away in retaliation. The spirits of the ancestors and gods, however, continued to move freely between the two realms.

On December 23 of the lunar year or whenever one of the kitchen gods gets broken, the clay figures are placed on their sides to rest. Incense is burned, along with ghost money and paper clothing. Sweet rice and fresh fruit are placed as offerings to the kitchen gods to speed them on their long journey back to heaven.

The next morning the old and broken clay kitchen gods are thrown away and replaced with new ones, but if the kitchen gods are not broken and have just been resting on their special day, they are turned back upright to hold the cooking pots for another year. More modern households now have metal racks that replace the clay kitchen gods, but Mai's mother still rests her pots on the clay figures.

BASIL CHICKEN

GA (CHICKEN) THONG (MIXED) RAU QUE (BASIL)

1 whole chicken breast, with skin
and bones

dash, freshly ground black pepper

salt, to taste

1 cup fresh Thai basil leaves (can
substitute rau ram or chopped,
Italian basil)

Ingredients for dressing:

1 tbsp. lemon or lime juice, freshly
squeezed

1 small garlic clove, smashed and
minced

1 tsp. sweet chili sauce (or substitute 1/8 tsp. crushed red
pepper)

1 tsp. sugar

2 tbsp. fish sauce

1 tsp. sesame oil (optional)

SERVES 2

1. Put the chicken in a large pot and cover with water. Bring to a boil; turn down heat and simmer, covered, for 20 minutes. Remove the chicken from the pot and let cool. Skin and bone the chicken and shred the meat onto a platter. Add pepper and salt to taste. Scatter the leaves or shreds of basil over the chicken.

2. Mix together the dressing ingredients and pour over the chicken and mix thoroughly. May be served warm or cold

This is an excellent and simple diet chicken recipe and can be served with **steamed rice (p.106)**, **pickled cucumbers (p.13)** or **salad.**

Thai basil, which grows year-round in Vietnam near the wells and cisterns, has a red stem and a more minty flavor than Italian basil. Rau ram is another leaf herb that can be substituted for Italian or Thai basil, but it has a distinctively bitter flavor.

Many Vietnamese herbs are used for both cooking and medicinal purposes, particularly for stomach and intestinal problems. Nothing in Vietnam is wasted. Spider webs are used as bandages; bitter melon is a treatment for high blood pressure, asthma, diabetes and constipation, and even a barnyard chicken can serve as a home remedy as well as a meal.

Mai liked to climb and pick the fruit in the fruit trees growing in her courtyard. She usually preferred the largest fruit furthest from the ground, and one day she lost her footing and fell to the hard ground below. Her mother quickly killed one of the chickens, split it open and wrapped and tied it around Mai's broken arm to reduce the swelling. While Mai spent the next several hours with a dead chicken wrapped around her arm, Mai's mother pounded leaves to make a paste that would serve as a cast and then wove bamboo around the paste to secure it. Mai would wear the cast for several months, but when it was removed, there was no swelling, and the arm had completely healed.

CHICKEN CURRY (DIRTY CHICKEN)

GA (CHICKEN) NAN (COOKED) CARI (CURRY) DO (DIRTY)

1 whole chicken (4 lb.)

3 large cloves garlic, minced

1 ½ tbsp. curry powder

¼ tsp. freshly ground black pepper

5 tbsp. fish sauce

1 tbsp. ginger root, minced

4 (2 ½ lb.) medium sweet potatoes
    or yams (regular potatoes can
    be substituted)

1 tbsp. cooking oil

4 cups water

2 stalks lemon grass, cut into 2"
    lengths

1 ½ cups coconut milk

garnish with:

chopped scallions

cilantro

Condiment:

1 tbsp. crushed red pepper (or 1
    fresh hot pepper, minced)

1 tbsp. rice vinegar (if using fresh
    hot pepper, substitute the juice
    of 1 freshly squeezed lime)

1 tbsp. salt

SERVES 6-8

1. Wash the chicken and discard the giblets. Cut the chicken into single portion sized pieces (wings, thighs, drumstick, breast, etc.) Be careful to cut at the joints so as not to get bone splinters. (You can substitute chicken pieces or have the butcher cut up the chicken for you.) Put the chicken into a large bowl.

2. Smash the garlic with the side of a knife and mince. Add the garlic to the chicken, along with the 1 ½ tbsp. curry powder, ¼ tsp. black pepper and 3 tbsp. of fish sauce.

3. Mince the ginger root and add to the chicken and mix the chicken and its marinade thoroughly together. Allow to marinate for at least ½ hour.

4. Put 1 tbsp. of cooking oil in a wok over very high heat. When the oil is very hot, put ½ of the chicken pieces into the wok, with the skin side down. Cook for 5 minutes on one side and then turn the pieces and cook for another 5 minutes on the other side until both sides are well browned. Remove the chicken pieces to a large cooking pot. Add the rest of the chicken, skin side down, to the wok and cook for 5 minutes on each side. Add these chicken pieces to the chicken in the large cooking pot.

5. Pour 4 cups of water into the wok and cook, stirring for 2 minutes, scraping the seasonings and mixing them with the water. Pour the seasoned water over the chicken in the large pot, and put the pot on the stove over high heat. Bring the pot to a boil.

6. Smash the lemon grass with the side of a knife and cut it into 2" lengths. Add the lemon grass to the pot of chicken, cover, and reduce the heat to a simmer. Simmer for 15 minutes.

7. Peel the sweet potatoes and cut them into 1 ½" cubes. Add the sweet potatoes to the chicken pot, cover and cook for ½ hour.

8. Just before serving, add 2 tbsp. fish sauce and 1 ½ cups coconut milk to the chicken, stir and heat through. Remove to a serving dish and garnish with chopped scallions and cilantro leaves.

9. For the spicy condiment: in a small bowl, mix the pepper flakes, salt and vinegar together and serve at the table, to be added to the chicken and sweet potatoes to taste. (If you use a fresh, hot pepper, substitute the juice of 1 lime for the rice vinegar.)

Serve with **steamed rice (p.106)** or **crusty French bread.**

This recipe is a traditional, Vietnamese curry with curry seasonings and coconut milk, but its name "dirty chicken" refers to a story of the third wife of a wealthy landowner in Quang Ngai, not the gritty texture the curry powder gives to the dish.

Preparing curried (dirtied) chicken.

The first wife of a wealthy landowner had no children, and so he took a second wife. The first wife, however, remained as the mistress of the household, while the second wife became the mother of the landowner's children and so had a special status of her own.

During a particularly bad harvest, one of the landlord's tenant farmers had no money or crops to pay his rent or even to feed his family. He did, however, have a beautiful daughter and offered her to the landlord as payment for his debt.

The rich landlord accepted the beautiful young girl into his household as his third wife, but she did not have the status of either the mistress of the house or the mother of the children, and the other two wives treated her badly and made her do all the most arduous household tasks, including most of the cooking. All the time she worked, they made fun of her clumsiness, messiness, ignorance, and stupidity, and when the two women sat down to eat, the third wife was only allowed the leftovers and the food that had fallen off or been discarded from the plates.

One day the third wife was cooking the chicken and sweet potato curry of this recipe when the first and second wife came by and taunted her as she worked. She was so upset that, as she stirred the pot of chicken and sweet potatoes harder, she knocked a piece of chicken out of the pot and onto the dirt floor.

"You clumsy, bumpkin," the first wife said. "You will have that piece in the dirt for your dinner, and that is all."

She and the second wife walked out into the courtyard laughing, and the third wife was so angry that as she continued to stir, another piece of chicken spilled out onto the floor. Realizing that she was wasting the precious meat of the noon meal, she bent over to pick up the chicken, dust it off and return it to the pot but then realized that, if she continued to spill the chicken onto the floor, the chicken would be hers to eat, and there would be little for the first and second wife.

The two older women came by the kitchen hut and again laughed at the third wife as she scooped up the chicken pieces from the floor.

"Look at how clumsy she is!" they exclaimed and then walked away.

The third wife stirred harder and harder at her pot until all the chicken had fallen to the floor, and when it was time to serve the curry, the first and second wife dined on sweet potatoes, and the third wife feasted on dirty chicken.

STIR FRY CHICKEN with FLAT RICE NOODLES

GA (CHICKEN) HU (OLD-FASHIONED) TIEU (LAUGH) XAU

Stir-fry sauce:

3 cloves garlic, peeled

½ tbsp. sugar

2" piece fresh ginger, peeled

2 tbsp. tamarind powder

dash ground black pepper

2 tbsp. ketchup

4 tbsp. soy sauce

3 tbsp. + 1 tsp. fish sauce

2 tbsp. hoisin sauce

For the noodles:

1 lb. flat rice noodles (Banh Pho)

10 cups water

1 tbsp. salt

For the stir-fry:

3 tbsp. canola or corn oil

2 eggs

1 lb. chicken breast, cut into match-
    stick sized pieces

1 bunch scallions, trimmed and cut
    into 2" pieces

2 cups shredded carrot

1 lb. bean sprouts

Garnish:

½ cup chopped cilantro

1 cup ground roasted peanuts

1 lime, cut into 6 pieces

nuoc cham

SERVES 6

1. In a large pot, add 10 cups of water and 1 tbsp. salt. Bring to a boil and add noodles. Boil for 3 minutes. Drain the noodles in a colander and run cold water over them for 30 seconds. Set aside.

2. In a blender or food processor, put 3 cloves peeled garlic, ½ tbsp. sugar, 2" piece of peeled ginger, 2 tbsp. tamarind powder and dash black pepper and blend together. Add the ketchup, soy sauce, 3 tbsp. fish sauce and hoisin sauce and blend again. Set aside.

3. In a wok or non-stick frying pan over high heat, add one tbsp. canola or corn oil. Break the two eggs into a bowl and beat in 1 tsp. fish sauce and a dash of black pepper with a fork. Pour the egg mixture into the hot frying pan, and then add the chicken, stirring and cooking for two minutes until golden brown. Spoon 2 tbsp. of the stir-fry sauce around the rim of the pan and mix in with the chicken and egg mixture for one more minute and then transfer the chicken and egg to a plate and set aside.

4. In the same fry pan or wok, heat 2 more tbsp. of cooking oil and then add the cooked rice noodles, coating them with the oil. Then add 4 tbsp. of the stir-fry sauce and mix well. Add the shredded carrot and bean sprouts and return the chicken to the pan and mix again thoroughly.

Turn the chicken and noodle mixture out onto a platter and serve with chopped cilantro, ground roasted peanuts, lime slices and **nuoc cham (spicy fish sauce; p.21)**.

STIR FRY BEEF with FLAT RICE NOODLES

XAO (STIRFRY) BANH PHO (NOODLE) (SOW BUN FU)

Ingredients for noodles:

½ lb. flat rice noodles (banh pho)

2 tbsp. sesame oil

1 tbsp. fish sauce

½ cup roasted and unsalted
  peanuts, ground

Ingredients for stir-fry:

1 lb. beef, sliced thin (chicken or
  pork can be substituted)

4 thin ginger slices, chopped into
  matchsticks

2 cloves garlic, minced

1 tbsp. soy sauce

1 tbsp. fish sauce

½ tsp. black pepper

2 stalks celery, sliced ¼" thick on the
  diagonal

½ lb. bean sprouts

1 ½ tbsp. cooking oil

1 tbsp. hoisin sauce

Serve with:

2 limes, cut in quarters

chives or scallions, for garnish

SERVES 6

1. For the noodles: Bring 6 cups of water to a boil in a large pot. Add the rice noodles and cook for 3-5 minutes. Drain the noodles in a colander. Pour the sesame oil and 1 tbsp. of fish sauce over the noodles and mix thoroughly. Just before serving, add the ground peanuts and mix again. (This noodle dish is good alone or served with any stir-fry. It has a light, sesame and peanut flavor.)

2. For the stir-fry: Slice the beef very thin. Slice the ginger and mince the garlic and mix with the beef. Add 1 tbsp. fish sauce, 1 tbsp. soy sauce and the black pepper to the meat mixture.

3. Wash and chop the celery. Wash the bean sprouts.

4. Put the cooking oil in a wok and heat until the oil is sizzling hot. Add the celery to the wok and stir-fry for 2-3 minutes. Scoop the celery to the sides of the wok and add the beef mixture in the center. Stir-fry for another 3 minutes until the meat is lightly browned. Add the bean sprouts and stir-fry for an additional 1 minute. Add 1 tbsp. hoisin sauce to the mixture and stir to mix.

To serve: Put the noodles onto a platter and spoon the stir-fry beef over the top of the noodles. Garnish with the chopped chives or scallions and arrange the lime slices around the edge of the platter. The lime should be squeezed on the individual portions, to taste.

Mai's maternal grandfather had three wives and seventeen children, whom he supported by raising goats, cinchona trees, and probably opium on a large tract of land in the mountains. The goats provided milk, and the bark of the cinchona trees provided quinine, which was used in treating malaria. The opium had a ready market throughout Vietnam but particularly in the major cities, and Mai's grandfather grew rich and adopted the dandified style of a French colonial plantation owner.

The mountain farm was worked by the Moi, the nomadic farmers who live in the mountainous areas of Vietnam and have maintained their own language and traditions that keep them almost completely isolated from the peasant farmers of the lowlands. The rugged mountains also provided habitat for many animals, including tigers. Mai's grandfather loved to hunt the tigers, and he proudly brought the tiger meat to Mai's grandmother to cook and serve. Mai's mother remembers the meat, mostly because of its strong and unpleasant smell and was grateful that her father was not a very good shot and tiger meat was rarely served.

Dressed in his khakis and pith helmet, Mai's grandfather once shot a tiger in the leg, and the enraged animal destroyed most of his crops, but his hunting expeditions finally ended when he aimed at a peacock and shot a Vietnamese man instead. Mai's grandfather went to jail for a year, and his wives and children were forced to pay reparation to the dead man's family. Having lost their land and no longer wealthy, Mai's mother and her siblings were forced to work in the rice fields of another family, and Mai's mother never forgave her father. When she married the oldest son of a rich landowner, she made sure that she would never be without land again.

STIR FRY BEEF with LEMON GRASS & RICE NOODLE SALAD

THIT BO (BEEF MEAT) XAO (STIR FRY) XA (LEMON GRASS)

1 ½ lb. steak (or any good cut
  of beef)

2 cloves garlic, minced

1 tbsp. ginger root, minced

2 stalks lemon grass, chopped

3 stalks scallion, chopped

1 tsp. black pepper, freshly ground

1 ½ tbsp. fish sauce

1 tbsp. soy sauce

2 tbsp. cooking oil

**Ingredients for Vietnamese rice
  noodle salad:**

2 cups bean sprouts

1 bunch cilantro

3 sprigs mint

5 sprigs basil

3 cups lettuce, shredded

1 large or 2 small cucumbers, sliced
  into matchsticks

½ lb. rice noodles

½ cup ground roasted but unsalted
  peanuts

1 cup **nuoc cham (spicy fish
  sauce; p.21)**

SERVES 6

1. Trim the fat off the steak and slice the steak into thin, 1" long shreds.

2. Smash the garlic with the side of a knife and mince. Peel and mince the ginger root. Add the garlic and ginger to the steak.

3. Cut the bottom ½" off the lemon grass and remove any dried outer leaves. Flatten the lemon grass with the side of a knife and chop it into very thin slices and then mince (makes about ¼ cup). Chop the scallions into small pieces. Add the lemon grass and the scallions to the steak.

4. Add 1 tsp. black pepper, 1 ½ tbsp. fish sauce and 1 tbsp. soy sauce to the steak and mix together thoroughly. Set aside.

5. Put 4 cups of water in a large pot and bring to a boil. Add the ½ lb. of rice noodles and cook for 2-3 minutes. Drain and allow to cool.

6. Assemble all of the salad ingredients individually on a platter (if you want your guests to assemble their own individual salads) or together in a bowl, with the noodles at the bottom.

7. Put 2 tbsp. cooking oil in a fry pan over high heat. When the oil is very hot, add the steak mixture with its marinade to the fry pan and stir-fry for 2 minutes. Remove the steak to a bowl or platter.

8. For individual servings: Put ½ cup cooked rice noodles in a soup dish or bowl. Add ¼ cup bean sprouts, ¼ cup shredded lettuce, a few slices of cucumber, 3-4 basil leaves, 3-4 mint leaves and 1 sprig of cilantro. Top the salad with ½ cup of the stir-fried steak, 1 tbsp. of ground peanuts and 2 tbsp. of **nuoc cham (spicy fish sauce; p.21)**, to taste.

Sharing food and family traditions.

BEEF and WATERCRESS SALAD

THIT BO (BEEF MEAT) XA LACH XON (WATERCRESS)

1 lb. beef, sliced thin

1" piece ginger root, cut in slivers

1 clove garlic, minced

1 tbsp. soy sauce

¼ tsp. freshly ground black pepper

1 tbsp. cooking oil

1 bunch watercress (if you cannot
find watercress, you can substitute Boston lettuce, sliced in
half along the rib)

1 tomato, sliced thin, for garnish

Dressing:

¼ cup rice vinegar

1 ½ tbsp. soy sauce

1 ½ tsp. sugar

1 tbsp. cooking oil

SERVES 4

1. Place the beef in the freezer for a half hour to stiffen it and make it easier to slice. Remove from the freezer and slice in very thin slices.

2. Cut the unpeeled ginger root into matchstick slivers. Smash the garlic with the side of a knife and mince. Add the ginger, garlic and ¼ tsp. black pepper to the beef. Pour 1 tbsp. of soy sauce over the beef.

3. Wash the watercress in a large bowl and then drain thoroughly.

4. In a small fry pan, pour 1 tbsp. of cooking oil. Turn heat to high. When the oil is very hot, add the beef mixture and stir-fry for 2 minutes until the meat is just cooked but still shows some pink. Remove the meat from the fry pan.

5. In the same fry pan over high heat, add the 1 tbsp. of cooking oil for the dressing. In a bowl, mix together the soy sauce, rice vinegar and sugar and add it to the oil in the fry pan. Stir to mix the ingredients and heat through.

6. Remove the dressing from the heat and pour it over the watercress. Stir to mix and then turn the watercress onto a platter, reserving the extra dressing in the bottom of the bowl. Place the sautéed beef mixture on top of the watercress. Garnish the salad with the thin tomato slices, and pour the remaining dressing over the entire salad.

This is a very quick, easy and light but tasty dinner. Serve with **French bread.**

Mai at the Asian market with lemon
grass and Thai basil.

SALTY PORK

THIT HEO (PORK MEAT) RAM (CARAMELIZED) MAN (SALTY)

1 ½ - 2 lb. pork tenderloins, cutlets
   or boned pork chops, cut into
   ¼" cubes (makes about 2-3
   cups)

2 cloves garlic, minced

2 tbsp. cooking oil

1 shallot, or small onion, minced

2 tbsp. sugar

¾ - 1 tsp. freshly ground black
   pepper

1/3 cup fish sauce

1 cucumber, sliced thin

½ cup ground, salted peanuts

cilantro, for garnish

SERVES 4-6

1. Cut the pork into ¼" or smaller, thin slices. (The smaller the pork pieces, the faster they will cook.) Smash the garlic with the side of a knife and mince. Mince the shallot.

2. Heat 2 tbsp. of cooking oil in a heavy fry pan over high heat until the oil is very hot and spitting. Add the minced garlic and shallot and stir until they have turned golden brown. Add the pork and 2 tbsp. of sugar and stir until the meat is well browned and has absorbed all the juices (about 15 minutes). The sugar should caramelize on the meat and pan, so scrape the pan as you stir.

3. Turn the heat off and add the fish sauce and stir until the sauce is absorbed by the meat. Add the black pepper and stir again.

4. Slice the cucumber in thin slices, on the diagonal.

5. Grind the peanuts and put in a separate bowl.

6. Put the salty pork on a large plate or platter and surround with the sliced cucumbers and garnish with the cilantro.

7. Serve with **steamed sticky rice (p.106)**. To serve, give each person a small bowl in which to put some sticky rice, pork and cucumber. Everyone can also add the ground peanuts, or using chopsticks or their fingers, they can pick up the rice with some meat or cucumber and dip it into the ground peanuts before eating.

This recipe can be decreased but not increased, because the pork will not cook to the proper, crispy consistency.

For a variation, add **½ lb. uncooked and unpeeled shrimp** and **1 tbsp. fish sauce** when the pork is cooked through and continue cooking and stirring until the shrimp has turned pink and is cooked through. Serve as above. Salty pork is also excellent served with **pickled cabbage** instead of the cucumber.

"Salty pork" is served throughout Vietnam. The dish actually uses no salt, but the fish sauce and pepper give the meat a distinctive, salty flavor. In Vietnam, the dish is cooked and served in a clay pot, and the diners scrape the bits of flavoring from the side of the pot as they eat.

Mai's mother always served this dish to friends and relatives who were new mothers, as the saltiness of the dish was supposed to help tighten up stretched muscles after childbirth, and the sweet rice, which is rich in vitamins, provided extra nutrition for nursing. The dish, however, is universally popular and can be served hot, at room temperature or cold for a picnic. It can also be reheated.

As well as a pet chicken, Mai had a small, pet pig as part of her dowry. She loved to feed and take care of the pig, but it failed to grow. One day when Mai had been a little too outspoken in school, her teacher came to the house to talk to Mai's mother about disciplining Mai. Mai hid behind the house, but the pig wandered out into the courtyard and proceeded to urinate on the bare foot of the teacher. Mai was not disciplined for her behavior in school, but the stunted pig ended up as salty pork.

PORK with LEMON GRASS

THIT HEO (PORK MEAT) NUONG (BARBECUED) VA (WITH) XA (LEMON GRASS)

2 stalks lemon grass, chopped fine

½ tsp. ground black pepper

2 large cloves of garlic

3 tbsp. cooking oil

2 tsp. soy sauce

2 tsp. fish sauce

2 scallions, chopped

2 tsp. sugar

2 lbs. pork loin

bamboo skewers

Garnish:

leaf lettuce, shredded

cucumber, sliced thin

1 cup fresh mint leaves

½ cup ground peanuts

SERVES 4-6

1. Soak the bamboo skewers in water so they do not ignite on the grill.

2. Slice the pork loin into thin strips.

3. Put the lemon grass, pepper, garlic, oil, soy sauce, fish sauce, sugar and scallions into a blender or food processor and mince. Pour the marinade over the pork strips and marinate for at least 1 hour or over night.

4. Thread the meat onto bamboo skewers and barbecue on the grill over a hot fire or broil them 6" from the broiler flame. Cook for 2-3 minutes per side.

Serve on a platter with garnishes and **nuoc cham (spicy fish sauce; p.21)**.

A whole pig roasting on a bamboo pole.

When Mai visited her village in 1993, she brought one of her brothers a 13 inch, black and white television that ran on batteries. Even in 1993, there was only one station, but most of the villagers had never seen a television set, so Mai's brother set it up in the courtyard of their home, and soon almost 100 people had gathered to watch the gray and flickering images on the screen.

When Mai's cousin Diem began cooking pork ribs on an open grill in the courtyard, she did not want to miss the television viewing, but the smoke from the fat dripping into the charcoal fire became so dense that no one could see the television. Eventually, Mai's brother and the villagers drove Diem out of the courtyard and back into the cooking hut with the rest of the women.

Like most of Mai's recipes, this recipe calls for a leaner cut of pork than the ribs used by her cousin, but the grill should still not be placed upwind of a television.

PORK, CABBAGE & RICE STICKS

BUN (RICE STICK) XAO (STIR FRY) THIT HEO (PORK)

5 oz. rice stick noodles (bun)

6 cups water

2-3 cups shredded cabbage

½ lb. pork, shredded

1 large garlic clove, minced

2 scallions, cut into 2" lengths

1 tbsp. cooking oil

2 tbsp. soy sauce

2 tbsp. fish sauce

½ tsp. freshly ground black pepper

1/8 tsp. crushed red pepper

fresh cilantro, for garnish

SERVES 2-3

1. Bring a large pot with 6 cups of water to a boil. Add the rice stick noodles and cook for 2-3 minutes. Drain the noodles in a colander and cut them into 3" pieces. Set aside.

2. Shred the cabbage and set it aside.

3. Shred the lean pork meat and set it aside.

4. Smash the garlic with the side of a large knife and mince.

5. Cut the scallions into 2" lengths and set aside for garnish.

6. Put a large fry pan on the stove over high heat. Add 1 tbsp. cooking oil and then the garlic and stir fry for one minute. Add the pork shreds and cook until the pork is cooked through (about 2 minutes). Add the soy sauce and fish sauce and stir again. Add the cabbage, and cook, stirring for another 2 minutes. Add the rice noodles, freshly ground black pepper and crushed red pepper to the fry pan and stir to mix thoroughly with the other ingredients. Shut off the heat and remove to a serving platter. Garnish with scallions and cilantro.

A wedding party in the rain.

In a Vietnamese country wedding, the groom, his father and eight relatives arrive at the bride's house with gifts of sweet rice, beans, tea, and nuts for the bride's family and gold wedding earrings, rather than a finger ring, for the bride. After asking the bride's parents for permission to marry and drinking tea, the groom, his family, the bride and eight of her relatives (excluding her parents) walk back to the groom's home to celebrate the marriage with as many different dishes as the groom's family can afford to prepare. A wealthy peasant family always serves a pig or at least a chicken.

Three days later, the bride and groom return to the home of the bride's parents to report on the success of the marriage and present them with the steamed head of the pig. If the groom suspects that his bride might not have been a virgin, he cuts off one of the ears of the pig before presenting it, but in the country, girls marry as young as thirteen to insure their innocence, and most women in Vietnam marry before the age of twenty.

OMELET

TRUNG (EGG) CHIEN (ROASTED)

½ cup ground pork (or cooked ham)

½ cup bean thread (Chinese vermi-
    celli), soaked in warm water
    and chopped

2-3 tbsp. wood ears, softened in
    boiling water and chopped

3 tbsp. fish sauce

1 stalk scallion, chopped

pinch, chopped red pepper

pinch, freshly ground black pepper

6 eggs

2 tbsp. cooking oil

SERVES 4-6

1. Pour hot water over the bean thread and soak for 10 minutes. Drain the bean thread in a colander and cut into bite-sized pieces.

2. Soak the wood ears in boiling water for 15 minutes. Drain and chop the wood ears into small pieces.

3. Combine all the ingredients except the cooking oil in a large bowl. Beat the eggs and other ingredients together lightly until the eggs begin to foam.

4. Put the 2 tbsp. of cooking oil in a large fry pan over high heat. When the oil is very hot, pour the egg mixture into the pan and turn the heat to low. Cover the pan and allow the egg mixture to cook, without stirring, for about 12 minutes.

5. Uncover the pan and turn the omelet out whole onto a platter. Slice it into 1 ½" squares to serve.

6. This omelet is great for a hearty breakfast or for a light lunch or supper. Serve with **steamed rice (p.106).**

A toasted omelet served with tea.

When Mai was young and single, she wore her hair long and straight, but when a Vietnamese woman becomes engaged, she pulls her hair back in a ponytail, and a married woman wears her hair wound into a bun. In Saigon, Mai abandoned those traditions, visited the hairdresser and the manicurist regularly and preferred the elaborate, teased coiffures of the 1960s.

When they married, Mai took Brian Donohue's surname, although a Vietnamese woman usually retains her maiden name. After the birth of a first child, the woman is called by the given name of the first child out of respect for her new status, and children in the same family are often given names that rhyme or have related meanings. Aunts, uncles and cousins call each other by their birth order number. Parents are considered number one; the first child's birth order number, therefore, is two, and subsequent children are called three, four and five. Mai is Auntie Number Four, although she was the third child in her family.

Mai's favorite omelet memory is from her honeymoon with Brian at her godfather's country cabin in the highland resort of Dalat. Each morning the newlyweds awoke to the smell of the charcoal stove and a fresh omelet being prepared by the cabin's caretaker.

STIR FRY EGG & CABBAGE

TRUNG GA (CHICKEN EGG) XAO (STIR-FRY) BAP CAI (CABBAGE)

1 clove garlic, minced

3 cups cabbage, shredded

2 stalks scallion, cut into 1" lengths

3 eggs

½ tsp. freshly ground black pepper

1 ½ tbsp. fish sauce

1 tbsp. cooking oil

SERVES 2-3

1. Mince the garlic. Shred the cabbage, and chop the scallions into 1" lengths.

2. Break the eggs into a bowl and add the pepper, fish sauce and scallions. Stir to mix thoroughly.

3. Turn heat to high under a large frying pan. Add the cooking oil and then the garlic and cabbage. Cook, stirring, for 2 minutes. Pour the egg mixture over the cabbage and continue to cook and stir, scraping the bottom of the pan to keep the egg mixture from sticking. Cook for another 2 minutes and serve hot.

Serve with **steamed rice (p.1086**.

This is a very quick and easy meal when you have a lot of cabbage and unexpected guests. It is light, flavorful and reminiscent of the filling for eggrolls.

In the village, Mai's family kept chickens for food, but both eggs and chickens were considered luxuries and were rationed by the Viet Minh. Mai learned early to take the eggs from the chickens, prick tiny holes at the ends and blow out the centers to make omelets for the children in her care. She carefully placed the empty eggs back under the chickens to be gathered up for the Viet Minh officials.

CURRIED SHRIMP on BREAD

CARI (CURRY) TOM (SHRIMP)

1-2 lb. medium shrimp in their shells

½ tsp. seasoned salt

2 tbsp. cooking oil

3 cloves garlic, minced

½-1 tsp. curry powder, to taste

2 tbsp. fish sauce

3-4 tbsp. coconut milk

1 loaf, crusty Italian or French bread

SERVES 4

1. Wash the shrimp and sprinkle with the seasoned salt.

2. Heat the oil in a fry pan. Add the garlic and stir. Add the curry powder and then the shrimp. Stir until the shrimp is cooked through and turns pink. Add the fish sauce and then the coconut milk. Stir to mix thoroughly and heat through and then serve immediately in individual bowls with the cooking juices. To eat, peel the shrimp and dip the bread in the juices.

This is the simplest and most casual of finger-foods to prepare and eat.

Serve with **salad**, for a light summer curry.

The tiger is native to the Southeast Asian peninsula, but today it is a rare and endangered species. The story about how the sea became salty, however, begins with a prince capturing a tiger while out hunting.

In ancient times, all the animals could speak, and the captured tiger begged the prince to spare his life and offered to grant anything he wished in return.

"But you have nothing that I want," the prince replied.

"Ah, but you are wrong," the tiger answered. "I have something very priceless, although it is very small."

The tiger showed the prince a tiny grindstone, which he could hold in the palm of his hand. When the tiger said, "Grind away, little stone," the grindstone turned and began to pour out a white powder. The powder had a sharp flavor, and the tiger explained that when the prince added the powder to his food, the taste would be unforgettable.

"When you have enough of the powder," the tiger cautioned, "you must say, 'Cease, little stone,' or the stone will not stop grinding."

No one else had ever seen or heard of such a stone or the powder it produced, and the prince became famous for the tasty banquets he hosted with all the dishes flavored with the mysterious white substance. Soon the prince had the little stone grind enough powder to sell, and the new seasoning quickly added to the wealth and the renown of his castle.

A foreign prince, who lived in a land on the other side of the ocean, heard of the little grindstone and the white flavoring it produced and decided to take his ship to see the magic for himself and perhaps buy some of the substance to bring back to his own country.

When the foreign prince arrived on the shores of the other prince's land, there was a great welcoming banquet. Having too much to drink, the prince with the magic grindstone, pulled out his little stone and ordered it to, "Grind away, little stone." Immediately, the stone began to turn and produce the white seasoning.

The foreign prince was amazed and having tasted the seasoning on the banquet food, he determined to steal the little grindstone when the prince was not looking and take it back with him on his ship.

When the foreign prince had taken the grindstone and was safely back at sea, he took the grindstone out from his vest and commanded it to, "Grind away, little stone," and the stone began to turn. After a few minutes, there was a small mound of white seasoning in the palm of the prince's hand, and the foreign prince decided that he had enough seasoning for now and that he would put the little grindstone away.

"Stop, little stone," the foreign prince commanded, but the little grindstone kept on grinding.

"I said, 'Stop, little stone,'" the prince repeated angrily, but the stone kept on grinding.

The prince became worried and offered a reward if anyone on the ship could get the little grindstone to stop grinding the white seasoning, which was now piling up and covering much of the deck of the ship. One by one, the crew of the ship studied the little grindstone and ordered it to stop, but the grindstone kept on grinding.

All night the grindstone ground on and all the next day. The sailors used buckets to pour the salt over the sides of the ship, but the little grindstone ground faster and harder, and the salt filled the cabin and made it increasingly difficult for the crew to move along the deck to trim the sails or alter course.

A great storm hit the ship on the third day, and the ship foundered and sank to the bottom of the sea. The foreign prince and the crew were drowned, but the little grindstone kept on grinding and is still grinding to this day, which explains why the sea water is so salty.

And the tiger turned the careless prince into a pelican, and so the pelican spends his days flying over the wave crested sea and diving deep into the waters in search of the little grindstone.

EASY FRIED FISH

CA (FISH) CHIEN (FRY) GON (CRISPY)

2 lb. whole fish (scup, bluefish, trout or any firm skinned, flat fish about 1" thick that will not fall apart during cooking; you can also use almost any fish steak, except salmon)*

2 cloves garlic, including skin but crushed

½ cup cooking oil

nuoc cham (spicy fish sauce; p.20)

SERVES 4-6

1. Clean and wash the fish, making sure it is free of scales but leave the skin intact. Dry the fish with a paper towel and score the body with a knife, making an X through the flesh and across the middle on both sides.

2. Heat the oil to 350 degrees in an electric fry pan or until oil is spitting over high heat on a stove. Smash the garlic cloves with the side of a knife and add to the frying pan whole (you will eventually discard the garlic, so it does not need to be peeled or chopped).

3. Lay the fish on its side in the frying pan (Use a large pot cover to partially cover the fry pan to keep the oil from splattering). Fry the fish on one side for about 15 minutes until browned and crispy. Turn the fish to the other side with a large spatula and cook, partially covered, for another 15 minutes.

4. Transfer the fish to a platter and pour the **nuoc cham** over the fish while it is still very hot.

To serve: Remove the meat from the bones of the fish with a knife and fork or by using chop sticks to pick up chunks of the fish meat.

The flesh of the fish absorbs the fish sauce for a very tangy flavor. The sliced cucumbers also absorb the flavors of the fish sauce and provide a crunchy, contrasting texture to the texture of the fish and rice.

Serve with **steamed rice (p.106)** and **sliced cucumbers**.

Appropriate types of fresh whole fish or fish steaks are always available in Asian or Portuguese fish markets.

Easy fried fish with nuoc cham.

Mai's village was twenty miles from the South China Sea, and the only fish the family ate were the fresh water fish trapped when draining the rice fields. Mai's family grew a type of rice called "red rice" that was planted in deep, fresh water. The fields were flooded by a stream full of catfish and other freshwater fish, including the tiny and colorful fighting fish, with their stripes of red, green and purple.

Before the fields were harvested, Mai's mother would cook a beef bone in charcoal and throw it into a small retaining pool at the edge of the fields. A day later, the bamboo gate of the pool would be closed, and the fields drained, leaving the pool filled with enough fish to feed the family for several weeks. Mai's two brothers loved to collect the fighting fish and watch their violent fight to the death, but Mai would collect and separate the fish in glass jars for the children to watch, folding and unfolding their colorful fins.

Banquet Dishes

These last dishes are particularly elegant and require more than average preparation. They are all, however, well worth the effort, as they are both beautiful in their presentation and delicious. Because so many of the ingredients are served fresh, the preparation time is mostly cutting and slicing that can be done ahead.

For lack of a better term, we have labeled these the "banquet dishes," for they are a feast served alone or on a table stacked with other imaginative preparations designed to entice the honored ancestors home.

Mai's paternal grandfather was the son of a wealthy landowner and had a private tutor in Chinese language, history and literature. He had one sister who was considered precocious and independent. She taught herself to read and write in Vietnamese and Chinese by hiding in the next room and listening to her brother's tutoring sessions. She eventually married and moved to Saigon, but when her husband died young and left her with two small children, she returned to the village.

The young widow worked hard in the rice fields she had inherited from her father, but although she was able to feed herself and her children, her life was difficult for the first year after her return.

After a year, the villagers began to notice that the young widow still worked hard in the fields, but in the evenings or at the market, she wore lots of gold jewelry. The jewelry eventually attracted a greedy landowner, who began to visit the widow and asked her the origin of all the gold.

"In my dreams," the young widow explained coyly, "I have been visited by spirits who have told me where to dig in my fields to find this gold. Every time they have told me where to dig, I have found gold until I really have more than I need, so I am anxious to sell my land and return to Saigon with my children."

The greedy landowner offered to buy the land immediately for an unusually large sum of money, and the young woman agreed to sell, drawing up the deed herself in the Chinese pictographs she had learned from the tutor.

When the widow returned for a visit several months later, she found that the greedy landowner had excavated half of her former land, found no gold and was very angry.

"You have cheated me," the landowner said and demanded his money back, but the widow did not want to return to the back-breaking work in the rice paddies or life in the rural village.

"The gold I wore was all fake and purchased in Saigon," she told him "but I did not force you to buy the land. You thought you were cheating a foolish woman, and we both got what we wanted and deserved. If you insist that I give back your money, I will tell everyone in the village how stupid, foolish and greedy you were to be duped so easily by a clever, young widow."

The landowner did not want to appear foolish before the whole village, and so he kept the land and said nothing more.

When her two children were grown, the widow returned to live in the village, but even in old age, she was considered too sophisticated and eccentric. When Mai's grandfather, father, and uncles were kidnapped and killed, the elderly woman was kidnapped with them and would be the only woman in the group killed by the Viet Minh that night.

DOWRY CHICKEN on a BED of WATERCRESS

GA (CHICKEN) HOI-MON (DOWRY)

3 Cornish game hens (about
    1 ½ lb. each) *

Marinade:
4 tsp. sugar
4 shallots, peeled
4" piece ginger root
2 large garlic cloves
1 tsp. freshly ground black pepper
6 tbsp. soy sauce
4 tbsp. fish sauce
2 tsp. five spices powder

2 bunches fresh watercress
2 cups cooking oil
1 cup water
4 tbsp. rice vinegar
4 tbsp. soy sauce
dash, freshly ground black pepper

*Mai uses Cornish game hens instead of chicken in this recipe, because the game hens more closely resemble the chickens in Vietnam. Vietnamese chickens are smaller than American chickens, and because they are allowed to run free and scavenge for food, they have more flavor and texture than American chicken. Frozen Cornish game hens are readily available in most supermarkets.

SERVES 6

1. Defrost the Cornish game hens by unwrapping and leaving overnight in the refrigerator or by putting in a large bowl and covering the hens with warm water. Rinse the hens thoroughly and discard the giblets.

2. Put all the marinade ingredients in the bowl of a food processor and process to mince and mix the ingredients.

3. Put the hens in a glass bowl or baking dish and pour the marinade over the hens, making sure that the marinade also is poured into the cavity of the birds. Cover with plastic wrap and allow the birds to marinate for at least 1 hour or over night.

4. Put 2 cups of cooking oil into a wok and heat the oil to very hot and spitting. When the oil is hot, remove the game hens from the marinade and put them into the hot oil, arranged so that half of each hen is well immersed in the oil. Cook the hens over high heat for ten minutes and then turn them with chopsticks or tongs and press the uncooked side down into the hot oil. Cook another ten minutes. Keep turning and cooking the hens in the hot oil for a total of 40 minutes. The skin of the birds should be dark and crispy.

5. Remove the hens from the hot oil and set aside to cool.

6. Pour all but 1 tbsp. of the cooking oil out of the wok.

7. Wash the watercress and arrange it on a large platter.

8. Cut each game hen in half and then again in quarters and arrange the meat over the watercress on the platter.

9. Heat the 1 remaining tbsp. of cooking oil in the wok and pour in the remaining marinade. Add 1 cup water, 4 tbsp. rice vinegar, 4 tbsp. soy sauce and dash of black pepper and cook, stirring for 5 minutes until the sauce is hot and bubbling. (Makes about 1 ½ cups sauce.) Pour the sauce over the game hens and the watercress.

This is a very elegant dish, but although the rice and watercress can be eaten with chopsticks, the hen should be picked up and eaten with fingers to get all of the meat off of the tender, little birds. Serve with **sweet or sticky rice.**

The game hens can be cooked ahead of time and reheated in a 350 degree oven in a covered baking dish. Assemble the dish and pour over the hot sauce just before serving.

This recipe can also be used for cooking duck. Instead of using fish sauce in the marinade, substitute 1 tsp. of sea salt. Roast the duck, breast side down, on a rack over a roasting pan filled with ½ cup water and placed in a 350 degree oven. Turn the duck and baste with the marinade every half hour. Roast for 1 ½ hours until the skin is browned and crispy. Cut the duck into bite-sized pieces and place the pieces on the bed of watercress.

Woman selling hot peppers, duck eggs,
ginger and chickens at the market.

Mai originally found this recipe in a book she borrowed from a distant cousin. Mai's mother could not read or write, and she considered reading books, particularly love stories, a waste of time, but Mai found several places in her house where she could read relatively undisturbed. Her favorite spot was in a dark corner of a back room where her mother stored big clay pots filled with the salted tuna that would drain and become the winter's supply of fish sauce. It was dark and smelled of rotting fish, but Mai could be fairly certain that her reading there would go undetected.

Mai's cousin's book was set in Chau Doc on the banks of the Mekong River in the south of Vietnam. The heroine was a poor, peasant girl who fell in love with the son of a rich landowner. His parents forbade them to marry, but they agreed to meet one last time in the moonlight by the banks of the river. The peasant girl knew she could never love or marry anyone else, so she decided to kill her dowry chicken and prepare a final banquet for her lover. The book then described in detail the preparations for chicken, and Mai, sitting in her dark corner alone, could almost smell the ginger, garlic, five spice powder, fish sauce and soy sauce of the marinade.

In the distance, however, Mai heard her mother calling for her. She did not answer until she looked up and saw her mother silhouetted in the light of the doorway. Mai quickly lifted one of the grass mats from the top of the fish sauce jars and tossed the book into the jar.

"What are you doing here?" Mai's mother asked impatiently.

"Just checking the fish sauce, Mother," Mai answered primly.

"Well, come along now. Didn't you hear me calling you?" Mai's mother turned back to the doorway and walked out into the courtyard, and Mai followed quickly.

When Mai returned later to retrieve the book from the fish sauce, the pages were all stuck together, stained and smelled of rotting fish. She would never find out what happened when the two lovers met to eat their final banquet together, and it would be years before she was able to replace her cousin's book with another, but she would later recreate the recipe for the peasant girl's dowry chicken.

QUICK PEKING DUCK

Ingredients for duck:

1 duckling, fresh or frozen

½ tsp. salt

3 tbsp. vodka

½ tsp. sugar

3 tbsp. soy sauce

2 thin slices of ginger root

½ cup water

Ingredients for pancakes:

2 cups flour

¼ tsp. salt

2/3 cup water

sesame oil

Ingredients for sauce:

2 stalks scallion, chopped

1 small clove garlic, minced

1 tbsp. sesame oil

½ jar (15 oz.) hoisin sauce

1/8 cup water

¾ tbsp. soy sauce

Fresh ingredients:

1 bunch scallions

1 bunch fresh basil

SERVES 3-4

For the duck:

1. Almost every American city has a "duck man" who sells already cooked Peking ducks that are as good as anything most cooks can prepare at home. The ducks only need to be reheated in a 350 degree oven for a half hour and then allowed to cool down another 15 minutes before carving. When reheating duck, be sure to put the duck on a rack in a roasting pan, so that the duck will not sit in its melted fat. To keep the roasting pan from smoking, add ½ cup water to the bottom of the pan.

2. If you cannot buy duck from a "duck man" or if you want to try making Peking duck yourself, the duck is not difficult to cook but does take a long time. It can be done ahead of time and reheated as above.

3. Defrost, wash and dry the duck thoroughly. Rub both the cavity and the outside with the ½ tsp. of salt and then rub it again with the 3 tbsp. of vodka. Hang it up over a drip pan for 3-6 hours. (Mai used to hang her ducks from curtain rods, but you can also place the duck in an upright rack over a drip pan.)

4. Preheat the oven to 350 degrees.

5. Place the 2 thin slices of ginger root in the cavity of the duck, and brush the duck inside and out with a mixture of ½ tsp. sugar and 3 tbsp. soy sauce.

6. Put ½ cup water in the bottom of a roasting pan and place the duck, breast side down, on a rack in the pan. Roast in the oven for 1 ½ hours, turning the duck and basting it with the sugar and soy sauce mixture every 30 minutes. The duck should be a deep brown and very crispy.

7. Remove the duck from the oven and allow to cool down for 15 minutes before carving.

For the pancakes:

1. Mix the 2 cups of flour and ¼ tsp. salt together in a bowl. Gradually pour in the 2/3 cup of water and mix it thoroughly with the flour and salt. Turn the dough out onto a flat surface and knead for 2-3 minutes until the surface has a smooth consistency. Allow the dough to rest for at least 15 minutes. (You can make the dough the night before and wrap and refrigerate it. The dough, however, must be warmed to room temperature before rolling out. Warming can be done in a non-stick fry pan or a microwave.)

2. Sprinkle a few drops of sesame oil on a smooth surface. Take a 1" diameter ball of dough and roll it on the surface in the sesame oil. Using a rolling pin, press down on the dough and roll it out as thin as possible without tearing.

3. Turn the heat to high under a large, heavy skillet (if you use a lighter, non-stick fry pan, keep the heat at low) and sprinkle the surface of the skillet with a few drops of sesame oil. Use a paper towel to spread the oil across the surface. Cook the pancakes for 1 minute on a side and then turn to cook the other side for 1 minute. The pancakes should just be beginning to brown. Remove the pancakes to an ovenproof dish and cover, so that the edges of the pancakes do not get dry and brittle.

Pancakes can be made a day ahead and stored, sealed, in the refrigerator.

Pancakes can be reheated in the microwave or in a covered, ovenproof pan in the oven (350 degrees) just before serving.

For the fresh ingredients:

1. Wash and dry the bunch of fresh basil and arrange in a shallow bowl.

2. Wash the bunch of scallions and cut off the roots. Cut off the top 1/3 of the scallion. Cut the remaining 2/3 of the scallion into 2" lengths.

3. Using a sharp knife, insert the point of the knife, with the blade facing upwards, about half way down the scallion piece. Bring the knife up, slitting the scallion. Rotate the scallion piece and insert the knife at the same level and again bring it up and continue until the top half of the scallion begins to fan out. Put the scallion fans into a bowl of cold water. The fanned tops will curl, making a decorative and handy brush for spreading the sauce on the pancakes.

For the sauce:

1. Chop the scallion, and mince the garlic.

2. In a small sauce pan, over high heat, add the 1 tbsp. sesame oil, garlic and scallion and cook, stirring for 1 minute. Add the soy sauce and hoisin sauce and stir to mix. Add water to thin out the sauce a little and cook for another 2 minutes. (If you are using the last of the hoisin sauce in a jar, use the water to clean out the jar before adding it to the sauce.)

To serve:

After the duck has cooled, use a sharp knife to remove the skin from the duck. Cut the skin into 2" strips and place the skin on a large platter. Cut off the legs and wings and place them on the platter. Slice the breast meat into 2" long slices and add that to the platter. Using a small knife, remove as much of the meat as possible from the duck and add the bits and pieces to the platter. Arrange the fanned, scallion slices around the meat on the platter.

Arrange the fresh basil and any extra scallion in a shallow bowl.

Pour the sauce into a small, serving bowl, and put the pancakes in a covered, serving dish.

To eat, select a pancake, and using the fanned scallion as a brush, brush the sauce across the surface of the pancake and then add the scallion to the top. Select a piece of skin and meat to put on the pancake and then top with a few fresh basil leaves. Roll up the pancake and eat. This is very elegant and tasty finger food.

Serve with **sweet or sticky rice (p.106).**

Peking duck served with pancakes,
scallions, and hoisin duck sauce.

This is Brian's favorite dinner, and Mai makes it every year for Brian's birthday. One afternoon in Saigon, however, Brian woke up from a nap and went out into their small courtyard to search for Mai. Mai had gone out to visit with a neighbor, but she had left behind two ducks that she had bought at the market that morning and planned to prepare for dinner the next day. Calling for Mai, Brian was startled when the two ducks came rushing out from behind a shed, squawking and trying to peck at him, and he quickly retreated.

The next evening, Brian and Mai dined on Quick Peking Duck and Duck Blood Soup, a delicious end to Brian's bird ambush.

VIETNAMESE "NOISY or HAPPY PANCAKES" with PORK & SHRIMP FILLING

BANH (CAKE) XEO (NOISY)

Ingredients for pancake batter:

12 oz. package of rice flour
    (Bo banh xeo)
2 tbsp. corn starch
3 ½ cups water
1 cup coconut milk
1 tsp. curry powder
½ tsp. garlic salt
4 scallions, cleaned & chopped fine

Ingredients for filling:

6 tbsp. corn or canola oil
1 lb. ground pork or pork loin, sliced
    thin (or substitute shredded
    turkey or chicken)
1 lb. fresh shrimp, peeled and
    deveined
1 large onion, peeled and chopped
1 tbsp. fish sauce
1 tbsp. soy sauce
2 cloves garlic, minced
½ tsp. freshly ground black pepper
1 lb. bean sprouts

SERVES 6

1. In a large bowl, mix together all ingredients for the pancake batter and then set aside for at least ½ hour.

2. Heat a non-stick fry pan to high. Add 1 tbsp. of corn or canola oil and then the pork, breaking up the meat to separate the pieces with chopsticks or a wooden spoon for about 4-5 minutes. Add the fish sauce and soy sauce, then the minced garlic, black pepper, chopped onion and shrimp. Cook for 3 minutes or until the shrimp turns pink. Stir in the bean sprouts and transfer all the ingredients to a bowl and set aside.

3. Clean out the fry pan and turn the heat back to high. Add 1 tbsp. of corn oil and heat to thoroughly coat the bottom of the pan. When the pan and oil are very hot, pour ¾ cup of the batter into the pan and twist the pan to coat the surface with a thin layer of batter like a crepe or an omelet. Cover the pan and turn heat to medium or low. Cook for 5-6 minutes, making sure the batter does not burn. Uncover the pan, and with a spatula remove the pancake to a plate and put ½ -1 cup of filling in the middle of the pancake and fold it over like an omelet. Repeat until all the batter and filling is used.

Serve with lettuce, cucumbers, mint, basil, cilantro and **nuoc cham (spicy fish sauce; p.21)**.

Happy pancakes are not difficult to make but need to be prepared individually at the last minute so are best for a group that enjoys helping with the cooking.

Once upon a time there was a farmer who had only one son. Concerned that he would not have enough descendants to burn incense at the home altar after his death, the farmer decided to marry his son off early to an older woman.

Several months after the wedding, there was no sign that the daughter-in-law was pregnant, and the farmer asked his son if he was doing his "husband's duty". It quickly became obvious that the son was not sure what that duty was. Pointing to a bull and a cow mating in the field, the farmer explained that the bull was "doing his husband duty".

"How do I know when my wife wants me to do my duty?" the son asked, and the farmer was not sure how to reply but finally said, "When her cheeks are bright red."

One day the farmer and his son were high up on the roof mending the thatch, and the son's wife was down below in the courtyard, cooking pancakes on a charcoal fire. When the son looked down, he saw that his wife's cheeks were bright red, and he quickly scrambled down the ladder and hustled his wife inside.

"Where are you going?" the farmer shouted, annoyed that he had been left to finish the roofing job alone. Several minutes later, however, his son's wife reappeared in the courtyard, smiling, and as she poured the pancake batter into the pan, it made a loud spitting noise. When the son came out of the house, she smiled again as she folded the pancake over the filling in a half-moon shape and served it with spicy fish sauce to her husband. That is how the "happy pancakes" got their name.

PAPAYA SALAD

GOI (SALAD) DU DU (PAPAYA)

1 green papaya (about 1 - 1 ½ lb.)

1 carrot, shredded

2 limes, squeezed (about 4 tbsp. juice)

5 tbsp. fish sauce

4-5 scallions

3 tbsp. cooking oil

1 clove garlic, minced

¼ lb. lean, boneless pork

½ lb. medium shrimp

½ tsp. salt

1/8 tsp. ground black pepper

1 package (½ lb.) shrimp chips (found in the Asian market)

2 cups cooking oil for deep frying

Garnish with 1 bunch of fresh cilantro.

SERVES 6-8

1. Peel the skin off the papaya and shred the pulp with a potato peeler, small grater or in a food processor. Pour cold water over the grated papaya and allow it to drain in a colander. Shred the carrots and add them to the papaya shreds. Set aside.

2. Squeeze the juice of the limes (about 4 tbsp.) into a small bowl. Scrape the lime pulp from the peel and add the pulp to the juice. Add 5 tbsp. fish sauce to the juice and set aside.

3. Chop the green part of the scallions into ¼" pieces. (Save the white part of the scallion for another recipe or chop it for a garnish.)

4. Heat the 3 tbsp. cooking oil in a small fry pan and add the minced garlic. Sauté for 1 minute and then add the chopped scallions, stir-frying until the scallions are limp but not browned. Remove from the heat.

5. In a small pot of boiling water, cook the boneless pork for 15-20 minutes. Remove from the water, cool and slice the pork into bite sized (½" by 2") slices.

6. In another small pot, boil the shrimp in water until they turn pink. Drain the shrimp and rinse with cold water. Peel the shrimp and slice each one in half, lengthwise.

7. Add ½ tsp. salt to the draining papaya and carrot shreds, mix and wrap them in a clean, dry towel. Squeeze the papaya and carrot in the towel to remove excess moisture.

8. Put the papaya and carrot shreds in a large bowl. Add the cooked scallions and garlic, the shrimp and pork. Spoon the lime and fish sauce over the fruit and meat mixture, add the freshly ground black pepper and mix thoroughly. Turn out onto a platter and garnish with cilantro.

9. Put 2 cups of cooking oil in a pot large enough for deep-frying, and heat the oil over high heat to very hot. Add the shrimp chips, a few at a time, and cook them until they puff up like potato chips and are barely browned on the edges. (This will take only about 10-15 seconds.) Remove the chips from the oil immediately to avoid burning and drain them on a paper towel. Pour the chips into a large serving bowl.

To eat, scoop a spoonful of papaya salad onto a shrimp chip.

This dish can be prepared ahead of time but should only be assembled just before serving to keep ingredients crisp and fresh.

Papaya salad with shrimp chips.

In Vietnam, papaya is usually harvested when it is still green, because the partially ripened papaya does not disintegrate with the fish sauce dressing. Papaya salad is finger food, but scooped into the hollow of the colorful shrimp chips, this becomes a memorable meal.

STUFFED STEAMED FISH with VEGETABLES

CA (FISH) HAP (STEAMED)

SERVES 4-6

Ingredients for fish and marinade:

2-3 sea bass or black fish, cleaned but not skinned and with head and tail

½ tsp. sugar

dash, ground black pepper

2 tbsp. fish sauce

1 tbsp. soy sauce

1 tsp. ginger root, finely chopped

2 cloves garlic, peeled & crushed

2 tbsp. rice wine or cooking sherry

½ tsp. hot chili sauce

Ingredients for stuffing:

½ cup ground pork

2 oz. water chestnuts, finely chopped

2 shallots or scallions, crushed and chopped

4 wood ears, soaked in boiling water and chopped

dash ground black pepper

1 clove garlic, crushed

1 small (1.8 oz.) package bean thread, soaked in hot water

Vegetable platter:

4 Chinese dried mushrooms, soaked in boiling water and sliced

2 scallions, crushed and cut into 1" lengths

½ tsp. ginger, cut into thin strips

1 tsp. sugar

2 small tomatoes, cut in half, squeezed of their seeds, and then sliced into ½" pieces

black pepper, to taste

2 tbsp. soy sauce

1. Clean the fish and dry it with a paper towel. Score the fish in an X with a knife on both sides. Mix together the sugar, pepper, fish sauce, soy sauce, ginger, garlic, rice wine and chili sauce for a marinade. Put the fish in an oval baking dish and pour the marinade over the fish and let marinate for at least 1 hour.

2. Soak the bean thread in hot water for ten minutes and then drain and cut the noodles into approximately 2" lengths.

3. In a bowl, mix together the ground pork, water chestnuts, shallots, wood ears, pepper, garlic and half of the bean thread.

4. Remove the fish from the baking dish and discard the marinade. Rinse off the dish, and place the fish back in it. Stuff the cavity of the fish with the ground pork and bean thread mixture. If there is extra stuffing, form it into meatballs and arrange them around the edge of the fish.

5. In a large bowl, mix together the sliced, dried mushrooms, scallions, ginger, sugar, soy sauce, tomatoes and black pepper and let them marinate for at least 5-10 minutes. Arrange the vegetables around the fish in the baking dish. Spread the remaining ½ package of cooked and drained bean thread around the fish and vegetables.

6. Bring water in a large steamer to a boil over high heat. (If you do not have a steamer, put a block of wood in the bottom of a wok or a pot large enough to hold the baking dish. Add 4-6 cups of water to the bottom of the wok or pot, and place the covered baking dish on the block of wood over the water bath.)

98

7. Cover the baking dish tightly with aluminum foil and place it in the steamer. Steam at very high heat for about 5 minutes and then lower the heat to simmer for another 30 minutes.

Remove the baking dish from the steamer and serve immediately.

In Vietnam, fish is usually served whole with its head and tail. The head of the fish is greatly prized and is always offered to the most honored guest.

When one of the young girls in Mai's village became engaged to the son of a wealthy landowner, the girl's father was very proud that his daughter had made such a good match and invited the boy's father for a fish dinner to celebrate the engagement. When the father of the groom reached for the fish head before the bride's father had offered it, however, the bride's father jumped up from the table in anger at this show of impatience and bad manners.

"I am the head of this household," the bride's father blurted out what was an unintentional pun, and the father of the groom was so embarrassed that he left the house and, shortly afterwards, called off the engagement.

Mai's mother told this story to her children whenever she served them fish, determined to prevent them from mistaking the protocol for serving fish heads and jeopardizing a good marriage proposal.

VIETNAMESE BEEF FONDUE

BO (BEEF) NHUN (DIPPED) DAM (VINEGAR)

Ingredients for fondue cooking broth:

1 ½ cups white vinegar

1 cup water

1 tsp. sugar

Ingredients for dipping sauce (or substitute nuoc cham (p.20):

2 cloves garlic

2 tbsp. sugar

1 tbsp. sweet chili sauce

1 can flat anchovies or 4 tbsp. Vietnamese anchovy sauce (bottled)

1 tbsp. fish sauce

½ cup water

3 tbsp. fresh pineapple, chopped into thin strips

juice of 1 lemon (about 1 ½ tbsp.)

Meat and vegetable ingredients:

2-3 lb. tender, lean beef, sliced very thin

1 large, red onion, sliced thin

1 large Spanish onion, sliced thin

2, 2" pieces of ginger, peeled and sliced into matchstick lengths

2 medium tomatoes, cut in half and sliced thin

2 heads, leaf lettuce

ground black pepper, to taste

1 tbsp. cooking oil

1 bunch mint leaves

1 bunch cilantro leaves

3 small, pickled cucumbers, sliced thin (see p.13)

2 star fruit or mango, sliced thin

Rice paper wrappers:

1 package of rice papers

2 pie plates filled with warm water

SERVES 8-10

1. Put 2 cloves of garlic, 2 tbsp. of sugar and the chili sauce in a mortar or food processor and mince or pound them to a paste. Add the anchovies and process or grind to a paste. Then add the lemon juice, water and fish sauce and mix well. Add the pineapple slices, mix and then set the sauce aside. (If you don't like anchovies, use spicy fish sauce, **nuoc cham (p.21)**, instead of this dipping sauce.)

2. Put the beef in the freezer until slightly stiff and then slice it into very thin slices.

3. Arrange the lettuce leaves from one head of lettuce on a large, serving platter. Add the tomato slices, sliced but uncooked beef, the sliced onions and the ginger matchsticks. Sprinkle the meat and vegetables with the cooking oil and black pepper and then cover the platter with plastic wrap until ready to serve.

4. Arrange the rest of the lettuce leaves, the mint, cilantro, pickled cucumbers, and star fruit or mango slices on another serving platter and cover with plastic wrap until ready to serve.

5. Put the vinegar, water and sugar in a saucepan and bring to a boil. Transfer these ingredients to a heated fondue pot.

6. Fill the pie plates with warm water and put the meat and vegetable platters, the rice papers, the pie plates and the fondue pot on the table, with the fondue pot in the middle and the pie plates at either end.

With a plate and a small bowl for some of the dipping sauce, each guest first soaks a rice paper sheet on both sides in the warm water in the pie plates and then puts the rice paper to soften on the plate. When the rice paper has softened and is pliable enough to roll up, put some slivers of ginger and onion into the fondue pot and then put a slice of beef and tomato on the end of a fondue fork and cook the meat and vegetables in the fondue pot for about 1 minute. Remove the meat and tomato and then the onion and ginger and place them on the bottom edge of the rice paper. Add any of the other vegetables and fruits you prefer. Fold the bottom edge of the rice paper up and then fold over the two sides, and roll the rice paper with the ingredients inside into a roll. Dip the roll in the dipping sauce or **nuoc cham (p.21)** and eat.

This is another elegant finger-food meal. Most of the preparation can be done ahead of time, but the cooking is done by each guest at the table. For a large group, it is better to have more than one fondue pot, and to insure that the cooking does not take too long, keep the water and vinegar in the pot very hot.

FRIED TOFU STUFFED with GROUND PORK

DAU HU (TOFU) CHIEN (FRIED) DON (STUFFED) THIT HEO (PORK)

3 medium tomatoes

½ lb. pork, ground

2 cloves garlic, chopped

2 stalks scallion, chopped

½" slice ginger root, peeled and
  chopped

1 lb. (2 packages) fried tofu (soy
  bean curd)

5 medium sized mushrooms

2 ½ tbsp. fish sauce

¾ tsp. black pepper

3 tbsp. cooking oil

1 tsp. sugar

1 cup chicken broth

¼ tsp. garlic chili sauce

Garnish with chopped,
  fresh cilantro.

SERVES 6-8

1. Put the ginger slice, 1 clove of garlic and the scallions in a food processor with a metal blade. Process until the ingredients are minced. Add the pork, mushrooms, ½ tsp. of black pepper and 1 tbsp. of the fish sauce to the food processor and process again until the ingredients are thoroughly ground and mixed. (If you have bought unground pork meat, it can also be ground with the metal blade of the food processor before adding the other ingredients.)

2. (If you have bought fresh instead of fried tofu, put two inches of cooking oil in a wok or pan and heat to very hot. Cut the tofu in half on the diagonal, into triangular pieces, and put the pieces into the hot oil and deep fry for 5 minutes or until golden brown. Remove from the oil and let drain and cool on a paper towel.)

3. Scoop a tablespoon sized hollow out of each fried tofu. Fill the hollow with a tablespoon of the ground pork mixture. Press the mixture into the tofu hollow, but let it extend out beyond the edge of the tofu.

4. Chop the tomatoes into quarters and squeeze out the juice and seeds.

5. Over high heat, put 2 tbsp. of cooking oil in a wok. Add the second clove of chopped garlic and stir-fry to brown. Add the tomatoes and cook for 3 minutes until the tomatoes are limp. Add the 1 tsp. of sugar and ¼ tsp. of pepper, 1 cup of chicken broth, 1 ½ tbsp. fish sauce and ¼ tsp. garlic chili sauce. Stir

together for another 3-5 minutes until the tomatoes have formed a sauce. Remove the sauce from the wok and set aside.

6. Heat 1 tbsp. of cooking oil in the wok over high heat. Place the stuffed tofu in the wok with the pork stuffing side down. Cover the wok and let cook for 2-3 minutes. Uncover the wok and pour the tomato sauce over the stuffed tofu. Then add the scooped out pieces of tofu to the wok and stir again. Cover and cook the tofu and sauce together over low heat for 10-15 minutes. (If you prefer cooking without oil, the stuffed tofu can be cooked in a steamer for 20 minutes. Remove the tofu from the steamer and put on a platter and pour the tomato sauce over the dish.)

Serve the stuffed tofu and sauce on a platter, garnished with chopped cilantro.

This is a very elegant and tasty dish for guests. It can be made ahead and refrigerated and then reheated.

Serve with **steamed rice (p.106)** or **French bread**.

Stuffed tofu.

Side Dishes

The most common side dishes for a Vietnamese meal are a salad platter and steamed rice. Like the spicy fish sauce, these two dishes can be served with almost anything and give the characteristic light and fresh flavor and look to the Vietnamese table.

The flooded rice fields of Vietnam.

In the cities, French bread often accompanies a meal, but dishes that need a contrasting, crisp texture are served with the deep fried, shrimp chips or the black, roasted sesame crackers. In the country, rice is the staple and is served steamed, fried, and soaked, pounded and reconstituted as rice papers and rice crackers. One of the smells that reminds Mai most of her home in Vietnam is the aroma of steaming rice, but no fragrance can match the perfume of the rice fields on a hot summer day.

During the rainy, summer months, the Vietnamese farmers have an abundance of vegetables in their home gardens, including eggplant, peapods, chopstick beans, asparagus and a variety of squashes. Carrots, radishes, cabbage, sweet potatoes and rice provide the staples for the dry and colder winter season in January and February.

STEAMED RICE

COM (RICE) TRANG (WHITE)

2 cups long grain rice (super grade,
  Jasmine White Scented Rice)
3 cups water
1 tsp. salt

SERVES 4-6

1. Put rice in a saucepan; add water and salt and bring to a boil over high heat. Use chopsticks or a wooden spoon to stir rice frequently to prevent from bottom sticking. Cook the rice uncovered over medium heat for 8 minutes or until the water is almost completely absorbed.

2. Stir again and cover. Turn the heat to low and cook another 20-25 minutes. Serve hot.

Leftover rice is good for fried rice dishes or may be reheated in the microwave on high for 1 - 2 minutes.

For **sticky or sweet rice**, reduce the amount of water to 2 ½ cups. After the water has come to a boil and cooked for about 5 minutes, turn the heat to low, cover the pot and cook for about 10 minutes more or until the water has been completely absorbed. Be sure to stir the rice, scraping the bottom of the pan to keep it from sticking and burning.

When shopping, uncooked sweet rice is called Gao Nep (raw glutinous rice), but in a restaurant, the cooked sweet rice is called Xoi Nep (steamed glutinous rice).

Generosity is an important tradition throughout Vietnam. Even the poorest peasant will take in a stranger and offer him whatever food can be spared, and good deeds become a legacy of good luck for the grandchildren and great grandchildren. In the countryside, even a beggar at the doorway is always given a half cup of rice or food that was cooked and leftover.

A very wealthy landowner in Thong An Ninh had 3, big and strong sons and 7, equally big and strong grand-sons, and he visited Mai's mother and asked her about the possibility of one of his handsome grandsons marrying Mai, who was small and pretty and already had a reputation in the valley as a fine cook. Mai's mother, however, surprised him by refusing the offer, explaining that the grandson was not the oldest son and that she would never let her daughter marry into a family that was so greedy and stingy.

This particular, wealthy landowner had openly boasted that he offered the beggars at his door 7 handfuls of rice, but Mai's mother knew that he stored his rice in a container with a very small neck, so that when the beggar reached in, he could only take out a few grains of rice at a time. Mai's mother did not want the bad luck of such boasting and greed to become the legacy of her grandchildren.

FRIED RICE

COM (RICE) CHIEN (FRIED)

2 tbsp. cooking oil

2 stalks scallion, chopped

4-5 cups steamed rice

1 cup chopped, cooked ham (or any leftover cooked meat or vegetables)

2-3 eggs

1 tbsp. fish sauce

½ tbsp. soy sauce

1 tsp. ground black pepper

SERVES 4

1. Heat 2 tbsp. of cooking oil in a large frying pan over high heat. Add the chopped scallions and the chopped meat. Add the steamed rice to the pan and cook for five minutes, stirring the mixture with a spatula to keep it from sticking.

2. Break the eggs into a bowl. Add the fish sauce, soy sauce and pepper and beat them together lightly.

3. Push the rice mixture to the sides of the pan and pour the egg mixture into the center. Mix the egg mixture with the rice mixture quickly by stir-frying with a spatula for an additional 2-3 minutes until thoroughly mixed, lightly browned and ready to serve.

This dish is always a good solution for leftovers.

Wild rice is considered a weed in Vietnam, and the workers in the fields pull out the wild rice stalks and toss them aside to make room for the more productive varieties of cultivated rice. More often than not, the wild rice will take root wherever it lands, only to be pulled up and tossed aside again.

Mai compares her own life story to the cycle of this common weed plant, uprooted, transplanted, tossed aside, only to take root again wherever she landed. Mai's story is not that unusual for the Vietnamese, particularly during the last century, and the heroine of the epic Vietnamese poem The Tale of Kieu was also a refugee and survivor .... "a small, frail skiff that rides the waves/ may float or sink as fortune dictate.......It is my part to play a drop of rain/ that falls at random as spectators watch."[1]

---

[1] *Nguyen Du, The Tale of Kieu, translated and annotated by Huynh Sanh Thong, Yale University Press, Copyright 1983. Lines 1957-1958, 1961-1962.*

VIETNAMESE SALAD PLATTER

RAU (GREENS) SONG (FRESH)

2 cups bean sprouts

1 bunch fresh cilantro

3 sprigs fresh mint

5 sprigs fresh basil

3 cups lettuce, shredded

1 large or 2 small cucumbers, sliced
   into matchsticks

½ lb. boiled rice noodles

½ cup ground peanuts

1 cup **nuoc cham (spicy fish
   sauce; p.21)**

SERVES 4-6

Most Vietnamese meals include a salad platter. Stir-fry dishes, cha gios, egg rolls and spring rolls can be wrapped in lettuce or served with side salad. The **nuoc cham** is served in a separate bowl to be added to taste.

The fields around Mai's family
home in Thong an Ninh.

QUICK SESAME NOODLES

DAU ME (SESAME OIL) BANH PHO (NOODLE)

½ package flat rice noodles (banh pho)

2 tbsp. sesame oil

1 tbsp. fish sauce

½ cup peanuts, ground

SERVES 4

Bring 6 cups of water to a boil in a large pot. Add the rice noodles and cook for 3-5 minutes. Drain the noodles in a colander, and then put the noodles in a large bowl. Pour the sesame oil and 1 tbsp. of fish sauce over the noodles and mix thoroughly. Just before serving, add the ground peanuts and mix again.

This noodle dish is good alone or served with any stir-fry. It has a light sesame and peanut flavor and is a nice change from steamed rice.

MIXED VEGETABLES

TRAU (VEGETABLE) TRONG (MIXED)

1 tsp. salt

1 small jicama, cut into matchstick slices

2 medium carrots, shredded or cut into matchstick slices

1 small cabbage head, shredded

½ lb. bean sprouts (optional)

1 bunch scallions, sliced and chopped

½ tsp. freshly ground black pepper

½ cup ground peanuts

5 stalks fresh cilantro (or 1 stalk of rau ram)

2 stalks fresh basil (or chives)

Ingredients for dressing (makes ¾ cup):

1-2 lemons, fresh squeezed for the juice (¼ cup juice)

2-4 cloves garlic, smashed

1-2 tsp. sweet chili sauce (or substitute ¼ tsp. crushed, red pepper)

¼-½ cup sugar

¼-½ cup fish sauce

2-3 tbsp. sesame oil (optional)

SERVES 6-8

1. Put 6 cups of water in a large pot with 1 tsp. salt. Cover and bring to a boil. Shred the jicama, carrots, and cabbage with a knife or in a food processor. Remove the cover from the pot and add the shredded carrots to the boiling water. Cook for 1 minute and then add the cabbage and the jicama. Cook for 2 more minutes. Add the bean sprouts and stir so that vegetables are immersed in the water. Finally, add the scallions, stir and then drain the vegetables in a colander. Squeeze out the excess water with your hands and put the blanched vegetables into a large bowl.

2. For the dressing, smash the garlic with the handle of the knife or grind in a mortar and then mix with sugar, lemon juice, chili sauce, optional sesame oil and fish sauce in a bowl or grind and mix in a food processor.

3. Sprinkle the vegetables with the ½ tsp. ground black pepper and then add the ground peanuts, cilantro and basil leaves. Mix thoroughly and then pour 8 tbsp. of the dressing over the vegetables and mix again.

Put the remaining dressing in a small bowl or pitcher to be added by those who want a spicier dish.

Can be served at room temperature or cold.

PICKLED CHINESE MUSTARD GREENS

CAI TAU (MUSTARD GREEN) MUOI CHUA (PICKLED)

2 - 2 ½ lb. mustard greens

2/3 cup white vinegar

3 ½ cups water

¼ cup salt

dash, alum

SERVES 8-10

1. Unlike the usual mustard greens, Chinese mustard greens have a thick stalk like a Chinese cabbage or celery, but the flavor of the greens is more peppery than cabbage. This recipe uses both the chopped stalks and leaves.

2. Mix together the vinegar, water, salt and alum in a saucepan. Over high heat, bring the vinegar mixture to a boil.

3. Wash the mustard greens and chop them into 1 ½" pieces and put them in a large bowl. Pour the boiling vinegar mixture over the greens and mix so that the greens are totally submerged in the liquid. Allow to cool and then transfer the greens to a large, covered jar. Press the greens down in the jar and pour the liquid to cover them. Allow the jar to sit at room temperature for 3 days before serving.

ZUCCHINI SALAD

BI (SQUASH) NONG (YOUNG) TRONG (MIXED)

4 medium zucchini (about 2 lb.)

1 ½ tsp. salt

1 bunch of chives, chopped in 1"
    lengths

¾ cup peanuts, ground

2 tsp. sesame oil (optional)

2 stalks, basil

½ tsp. freshly ground black pepper

SERVES 4-6

1. Slice the zucchini into thin (1/8") rounds.

2. Bring 3 cups of water and a tsp. of salt to a boil in a medium pot. Add the zucchini to the boiling water and cook until the water returns to a boil. Drain the zucchini in a colander and squeeze out as much remaining liquid as you can.

3. Put the zucchini in a bowl and mix with the chopped chives, ground peanuts, ½ tsp. salt, sesame oil, pepper and basil leaves and mix thoroughly.

Serve with toasted **rice/sesame crackers** or **shrimp chips.** To toast the sesame crackers, put one cracker at a time in the microwave and microwave at high heat for 1 minute. The shrimp chips are prepared by dropping them in very hot oil and deep-frying for a few minutes until they puff up like potato chips. Remove the shrimp chips from the oil and allow to drain on a paper towel.

In serving, scoop the salad onto a piece of the crackers or chips.

Zucchini salad with toasted sesame crackers.

Mai calls this dish "Vietnamese peasant food" because most families in the country grow their own peanuts, herbs and several varieties of squash, and during the rainy, summer months, the squash is particularly abundant. In preparing blanched, steamed or boiled vegetables, Mai usually drains and then squeezes them of excess moisture with her hands, so that the vegetables will absorb the flavors of the dressings.

STIR FRY CURRIED EGGPLANT

CARI (CURRIED) CA VI VE (EGGPLANT)

3 small eggplant (Chinese eggplant are more tender, but you can substitute regular eggplant.)

½ tsp. salt

2 cloves garlic, minced

2 medium tomatoes

1 medium onion

3 tbsp. cooking oil

1 ½ - 2 tsp. curry powder

1 cup water

¼ - ½ tsp. crushed red pepper

2 tbsp. fish sauce

1 tbsp. soy sauce

½ cup coconut milk (canned)

1 tsp. sugar

1 tbsp. chopped chives or scallions for garnish

SERVES 6

1. Cut the eggplant into large pieces (1" by 2") and put the pieces in a bowl. (Do not peel the eggplant.) Add ½ tsp. of salt and then cover the eggplant with water. The salt will keep the eggplant from turning brown.

2. Cut the tomatoes in half and squeeze out the seeds and extra juices. Cut the tomato into cubes.

3. Smash the garlic with the side of a knife and mince.

4. Cut the onion into large (1 ½") chunks.

5. Heat 3 tbsp. cooking oil in a wok over high heat until the oil is very hot. Add the garlic.

6. Drain the eggplant and add it to the wok. Stir. Add the 1 ½ - 2 tsp. curry powder and stir again. Add the onion and crushed red pepper and then pour 1 cup of water over the eggplant mixture and stir to mix. Cover the wok and allow to cook for 10 minutes.

7. Uncover the wok and add the fish sauce, soy sauce, tomatoes and sugar. Stir. Open the can of coconut milk and stir it if it has separated. Pour ½ cup coconut milk into the wok, mix thoroughly and heat through.

8. Remove the eggplant to a platter and garnish with chopped chives or scallions.

Serve with **steamed rice (p.106)**.

This is a great dish for vegetarians or curry lovers. The eggplant absorbs the curry and coconut flavors but does not get mushy. Leftover coconut milk can be stored in plastic freezer bags and frozen indefinitely.

STEAMED EGGPLANT

HO HAP (STEAMED) CA VI VE (EGGPLANT)

5 small eggplant (can substitute Italian eggplant, but Chinese eggplant are more tender, and if you use larger eggplant, you should increase the cooking time.)

1 tbsp. chopped chives

1 clove garlic

15 fresh basil leaves

1 ½ - 2 tbsp. fish sauce

¼ tsp. chopped red pepper

SERVES 4

1. Fill the bottom of a steamer or wok with 3 cups of water and turn heat to high. Cut the stem ends off the eggplant and place the eggplant, whole, in the top of the steamer or on a rack or plate in the wok. Cover and steam for 30 minutes.

2. Chop the chives into ¼" pieces.

3. Smash the garlic with the side of a knife and mince.

4. Remove the eggplant from the steamer and allow to cool enough to handle. Using the tip of a knife, peel the skin off the eggplant and discard it. Shred the eggplant pulp with a fork and put the shredded pulp in a bowl. Add the minced garlic and chopped chives. Chop the basil leaves into small pieces and add them to the eggplant. Add the chopped red pepper and the fish sauce and mix thoroughly.

Serve with **barbecued chicken breast (p.58)**

This is a very simple but tasty peasant dish. It can be served hot or cold.

In the countryside, where a farmer might not have a steamer, the eggplant would be placed to steam on top of the rice after cooking. The eggplant can also be cooked over a hot grill and then peeled.

EGGPLANT STEAKS

CA VI VE (EGGPLANT) NUONG (GRILLED)

2 medium eggplant

5 tbsp. cooking oil

2 tbsp. basil, minced

2 tbsp. chives, minced

5 tbsp. **nuoc cham (spicy fish sauce; p.20)**

SERVES 4-6

1. Do not peel the eggplant, but cut off the top and bottom and then slice the eggplant into ½" thick, round steaks. Brush both sides of the eggplant slice with cooking oil and place on a hot grill for about 5 minutes on each side (or place under a hot broiler for 5 minutes on each side). Remove and place on a platter.

2. Mince the basil and chives and sprinkle them across the tops of the eggplant steaks. Spoon the spicy fish sauce over the eggplant and serve.

These eggplant steaks can be served as a vegetarian main dish or as a side dish. They should be spicy and salty. Serve with **steamed rice (p.106)** to soak up the juices or **French bread**.

Desserts

Most Asian desserts are too sweet for American tastes, but Mai likes to finish an evening with a Vietnamese fruit compote, which is light and refreshing. In Vietnam, most fruits would be served fresh, but the jackfruit, rambutan, longan and lychees are difficult to find in American markets. Because these tropical fruits all have good texture and flavor, the canned varieties are a good substitute.

In Saigon, desserts mostly reflect the influence of the French. There are many, small French pastry shops in the city, and an elegant meal in a home or a restaurant would frequently end with a traditional flan or a selection of French pastries.

Baskets of fresh produce at an open market,
including tomatoes, scallions, onions,
limes, and pineapple.

FRUIT COMPOTE

TRAI (FRUIT) CAY (TREE)

3-5 cups ice cubes (or ½ of a 5 lb. bag of ice)

1 pt. fresh strawberries, cut in half

1 (1 ¼ lb.) can lychees

1 (1 ¼ lb.) can jackfruit

1 (1 ¼ lb.) can rambutan

1 (1 ¼ lb.) can longan

1 (11 oz.) can mandarin oranges

SERVES 15-20

1. Fill a very large bowl with ice cubes.

2. In a separate bowl, mix together the fruit and liquid from the cans of lychees, jackfruit, rambutan, longan and mandarin oranges. Add the sliced strawberries.

3. Stir to mix and then pour the fruit over the ice. Serve very cold.

This is a very simple but tasty and attractive dessert for a large gathering. As the ice melts and mixes with the fruit juices, the cool liquid is especially refreshing after a big and filling meal. Mai adds strawberries to the otherwise Asian dish to provide color.

In Vietnam, tropical fruits are abundant and sometimes serve more than one use. The juice of the tropical fruits and coconuts are particularly welcome in the hot climate, and fruit snacks can easily be picked from the trees just before eating.

The tender young orange, lemon and banana leaves are used for wrapping fish, pates and other delicate foods for grilling, and when a young woman dies during pregnancy or childbirth, a banana tree is planted at the foot of her grave. When it first blooms, she and the baby are considered ready for reincarnation.

The jackfruit has cool and juicy fruit inside, but the outside is protected by a thick and spiny skin. When Mai was late for school, her teacher sometimes punished her by making her kneel on the skin of the jack fruit in front of the class, but that punishment did little to spoil her appetite for the sweet and tasty fruit.

PEANUT SESAME CANDY

ME (SESAME) XUONG (SWEET)

1 cup sesame seeds, lightly toasted
    in the broiler or toaster oven

1cup salted and roasted peanuts

4 cups sugar

1 cup water

1 cup white vinegar

butter to grease the pan

SERVES 6

1. Toast the sesame seeds. Put the sugar, water and vinegar in a medium saucepan over high heat and bring to a boil. Boil for 5 minutes. Turn the heat down to simmer for another minute until the mixture is thick and gooey. (It should form a ball when dropped into a cup of cold water.)

2. Grease the bottom of an 8" square pan with butter and sprinkle half of the sesame seeds and half of the peanuts across the bottom of the pan. Pour the sticky sugar-vinegar over the peanuts and seeds and then cover with the remaining sesame seeds and peanuts. Allow to cool.

This is a very sticky and difficult to serve dessert, but it is a delicious combination of sweet and sour. Scoop it out with a teaspoon and eat it with your fingers or serve it in small, muffin doilies.

When Mai's mother was pregnant with her third child, Mai's father took a second wife from the region of Binh Dinh, about 75 miles south of Mai's village. Although second wives were a sign of affluence and prosperity in Vietnam, Mai's mother did not appreciate sharing her husband with a younger woman, and when the second wife came to visit with gifts of this sticky candy for the children, Mai's mother stood behind and pinched them to keep them from accepting the offering. Although she had no choice in sharing her husband's affection, she did not want to share the affection of her children.

COCONUT CANDY STRIPS

MUC (CANDY) DUA (COCONUT)

2 fresh whole coconuts

1 cup water

½ cup sugar

food coloring

(DESSERT OR SNACK)

1. Open the coconuts, drain the milk and remove the meat in large chunks. With a potato or carrot peeler, shave the coconut into slivers about 1" to 2" long (or use the shredder attachment in a food processor). You should have about 1 cup shredded fresh coconut.

2. In a large, heavy saucepan, heat the water and ½ cup of sugar. Add a few drops of food coloring to the sugar and water if you want a more colorful candy. (Red or green for the holidays, etc.) Bring to a boil and add the coconut. Stir the coconut in the boiling mixture until the sugar and water are reduced to a syrup consistency. Lower the heat and keep on stirring until the mixture dries and coats the coconut strips. If the heat is too high, the mixture will caramelize and brown the coconut.

3. Remove the sugared coconut strips from the heat and allow to cool on a clean cookie sheet.

Clean the pan thoroughly while it is still warm or before repeating the process for another batch of coconut.

The coconut candy is a wonderful, holiday treat and remains fresh for weeks.

The weeks just before Tet, the lunar new year and biggest holiday in Vietnam, are the busiest of the year. Debts must be paid off, friendships mended, graves of the ancestors swept clean, clothes washed and repaired, and all the foods for the first three days of the holiday prepared.

Although Tet continues for ten days, a fire is kept burning to offer both light and hospitality for the first three days, and visits are planned to the families of the oldest brother or the parents to worship together and celebrate the new year.

The first guest on the first day of the holiday is a specially invited man or boy, a first son or a particularly wise man who brings luck for the year when he enters the household before the others.

After that honored guest leaves, the family members arrive with gifts of candy, tea, cookies, incense, sweet rice cakes and fruit, and the grandparents give red envelopes with small amounts of shiny, new money to each of the children. Houses and shops are decorated in red, and watermelon seeds dyed red are the favorite snack of the season.

Gifts of food are always offered first to the ancestors and then are shared among the steady stream of relatives and guests.

When Mai asked one of her aunts why the ancestors were always offered the food first although these spirits never seemed to eat anything, the aunt scolded her for asking such a foolish question but assured her that the answer would become more obvious when she was older.

The only time Mai remembers an interruption in the usual peace and harmony of the Tet celebrations was during the Viet Cong Tet Offensive in 1968 when the sky over even the smallest hamlets was illuminated by gunfire instead of the usual fireworks. Mai's home in Thong An Ninh was destroyed and rebuilt several times between 1945 and 1970, but she always remembers that the Tet holiday was a brief respite from the hardships of the daily routine and war.

FLAN

¾ cups sugar

¼ cup water

12 oz. can evaporated milk

14 oz. can sweetened condensed
    milk

14 oz. whole milk

4 eggs

1 tsp. vanilla extract

You will also need:

steamer

electric mixer

4 cup steel or heat-resustant bowl
    (or individual flan/soufflé
    bowls)

SERVES 8

1. Put the ¾ cups sugar and ¼ cup water in a small saucepan over high heat. Bring to a boil and allow to bubble at high heat until the mixture cooks down and begins to caramelize and turn golden (about 5 minutes). Once the mixture begins to caramelize and turn golden, stir continuously to avoid scorching and continue to cook until all the sugar is a dark golden color (about 1-1 ½ minutes). Pour the caramelized sugar into a 4 cup steel or pyrex bowl (or individual, heat-tolerant containers). Rotate and tip the bowl to coat the inside surface completely with the caramelized sugar. Set aside.

2. Pour the evaporated, condensed and whole milk into a large mixing bowl. Add the eggs and the 1 tsp. vanilla. With an electric mixer, mix at medium speed for 2 minutes.

3. Pour the milk mixture into the bowl coated with caramelized sugar. Cover the bowl tightly with aluminum foil.

4. Put approximately 1" of water into the bottom of a steamer. Place the bowl with the flan mixture in the steamer. Cover the steamer and turn the heat to high for 5 minutes; then turn the heat down to medium and steam for another 30 minutes. The flan should be firm.

5. Remove the flan from the steamer and allow to cool.

To serve, unmold the flan onto a serving dish with the caramelized surface on top. Serve at room temperature or chilled.

This recipe can be made the day before and kept refrigerated.

Flan is a traditional French dessert. Like their baguettes, the French brought flan to colonial Vietnam, and it is still served in elegant Vietnamese restaurants and homes almost as frequently as it is served in Paris.

BLACK BEANS & SWEET RICE

¼ lb. dried black beans

1" piece of ginger, unpeeled

¾ cups sweet rice

3 tbsp. sugar

coconut milk (or banana leaves for
   wrapping)

SERVES 6

1. Soak the black beans in warm water over night.

2. Drain the black beans. Smash the ginger with the handle of a knife and put the beans and the ginger in a medium saucepan with 2 cups of water. Bring to a boil over high heat and then lower the heat to a simmer for 30 minutes. (Add more water if it boils down completely.) Remove the ginger and add ¾ cups sticky or sweet rice and 3 tbsp. of sugar. Add another 1 ½ cups water and bring to a boil and then reduce the heat, cover the saucepan and let cook for another 20 minutes. The water should be completely absorbed, and the mixture should be sticky and thick.

3. Scoop a ½ cup serving onto dessert plates. Open and stir the coconut milk and pour over the bean/rice mixture. (Or spoon the bean/rice mixture onto a banana leaf. Roll the leaf and secure with a toothpick. A few minutes before serving, steam the stuffed banana leaves and then serve warm.)

Index of Asian Ingredients

Alum powder: A preservative, available in grocery stores, that maintains crispness during pickling. It can be toxic when used in large quantities (more than 1 oz.)

Bamboo Shoots: A reedy vegetable, available canned.

Banana Leaves: The large, broad leaves of the banana tree, used for wrapping and grilling meats and fish and available frozen in Asian markets. Banana leaves can be defrosted by allowing them to sit on a counter for a half hour or by rinsing in warm water before using.

Thai Basil: Has a smaller leaf, a red stem and a more minty flavor than Italian basil. Italian basil can be used as a substitute but is best when mixed with some mint.

Bean Sprouts: Just sprouted mung beans. Buy fresh bean sprouts or sprout your own mung beans by washing the beans daily with water and then draining until sprouts begin to appear. Canned bean sprouts are limp and soggy.

Bitter Melon: Looks like a shriveled cucumber and is used in soups, salads or stir fried with egg. The melon is considered medicinal, keeps its firm texture when cooked and has a very mild but distinctly bitter flavor.

Chili Sauce: Comes in several varieties. They all provide a spicy, hot pepper flavoring, but the sweet chili sauce or chili sauce for chicken has added sugar, whereas the chili sauce with garlic does not. Hot red pepper flakes can be substituted.

Chopsticks: In Vietnam, chopsticks are used for cooking, eating and serving. In cooking, the chopsticks are useful for separating bits of meat or vegetables. At the table, the Vietnamese eat with the small end of the chopsticks, but rotate the chopsticks to use the large end for selecting food from the serving dishes.

Cilantro (Coriander): A pungent flavored herb which resembles parsley in appearance. The leaves are used frequently in Asian cooking as well as in Mexican and European cooking. The seeds are also used dried and ground.

Coconut Milk: Fresh milk from the coconut used in curries. Canned coconut milk is readily available and a convenient substitute for fresh. The milk is apt to separate in the can and should be stirred before using.

Corn Starch: Used occasionally in Vietnamese cooking for thickening. Mix first with water to avoid lumps.

Curry Powder: There are lots of Asian curry powders available, but Mai's favorite is Golden Bell Curry.

Eggroll or Wonton Skins: A thin, wheat pastry used as wrappers for eggrolls or wontons, available fresh or frozen in Asian market refrigerators.

Fish Sauce (nuoc mam): Bottled fish extract is the most common flavoring ingredient in Vietnamese cooking.

Rambutan, jackfruit, and lychees in the market.

Depending upon the region of the country, fish sauce is extracted from anchovies, tuna, cuttlefish or whatever is readily available. Good fish sauce is usually more expensive than average varieties, but a good fish sauce in Vietnamese cuisine is prized like a good wine in French cooking. The best fish sauce comes from the island Phu Quoc in the Gulf of Thailand, off the southwest coast of Vietnam.

Five Spice Powder: A mixture of five, aromatic, dried spices (ground star anise, cloves, Chinese cinnamon, Szechuan peppercorns and fennel seed) available in small spice jars or packets in Asian markets.

Ginger Root: A tuberous root with a brown skin used for flavoring. The root is usually peeled and chopped finely or mashed. Fresh ginger is much stronger than powdered ginger.

Hoisin Sauce: Thick, brown paste sauce used alone or as pungent flavoring in sauces.

Jackfruit: The Jackfruit tree is native to Southeast Asia and produces large fruits with a prickly exterior rind. The numerous interior bulbs are very sweet when ripe.

Jicama: A large, mild flavored, root vegetable, often used in Mexican cooking and sometimes called a Mexican potato.

Lemon Grass: A long, slender and tough green grass with a strong lemon flavor and aroma when cooked. The soft, central pulp is used for soups and marinades. To use, cut off the stem end and remove any dried-out outer layer. Pound the central stem with the butt of a knife, a pestle or a tenderizing hammer. Chop the pulp into small pieces. Lemon grass grows well in the garden but is not winter hardy in the North. To store lemon grass, chop the stalks into 3" pieces, put in a plastic, freezer bag and store in the freezer.

Lychee: A tropical fruit native to China with a delicate translucent pulp with a fragrant and sweet fruit.

127

Pho and its accompanying salad platter.

Mango: A tropical fruit with a citrus flavor.

Mustard Greens: Chinese mustard greens have the same peppery flavor of other mustard greens, but they have a thicker, celery-like stalk.

Noodles: Asian markets offer a huge variety of noodles. Several types of transparent noodles are called Chinese vermicelli. **Bean thread** is a transparent, very thin noodle made from soy beans. **Rice noodles** are produced in various shapes and sizes and are also called Chinese vermicelli but are produced from rice. The round rice noodles are called *bun,* and the flat rice noodles are called *banh pho.* To distinguish between the bean thread and rice noodles, you have to check the packaging. They look similar and both cook very quickly in boiling water and give texture to the dish as well as absorbing the flavors of the other ingredients. The ***fine vermicelli noodles*** require almost no cooking. They can be soaked in a bowl of hot water for 3-5 minutes and then microwaved for 1 minute to heat or put in a steamer or a basket on top of boiling water for 2 minutes to warm. Adding some oil and mixing after cooking will prevent the noodles from sticking to each other. Asian markets also carry **wheat noodles** that are usually flat and white but not translucent. These noodles are similar to Italian pasta and are cooked for several minutes in boiling water and drained like pasta. ***Egg noodles*** are also available refrigerated in Asian markets and are similar to fresh Italian pasta. They are used frequently in soups. Both wheat and egg noodles have more body and flavor and are more filling than the vermicelli noodles.

Okra: Okra is a plant in the mallow family cultivated for its edible seed pods, which are low in calorie and rich in vitamin C.

Papaya: A tropical fruit, with the consistency of a nectarine and a citrus flavor. The Vietnamese usually serve their papaya when the pulp is green and crisp.

Peanuts: Peanuts are used frequently in Vietnamese cooking to add flavor, protein and crunch to a dish. Unless otherwise noted, use unsalted peanuts.

Plantain: Looks like a banana but is greener. The pulp is firmer, drier and less sweet than banana. Plantains are available in any store offering tropical fruits or Southeast Asian or Mexican foods.

Radish Roots: A mild root which looks like a white carrot.

Rambutan: The rambutan is a tropical fruit with red or yellow skin and spines. The fruit inside is translucent and sweet like a grape.

Pho (sometimes called Pasteur Pho): The quintessential Vietnamese, heavily perfumed, beef broth soup served for breakfast, lunch and dinner by street vendors, restaurateurs and home cooks throughout Vietnam.

Rice: Whenever possible, rice should be as fresh as possible. Fresh rice is starchier and has more flavor. *Jasmine rice* is available in most Asian markets and health food stores. It is a long grain, white rice of good quality and flavor. *Sweet* or *sticky rice* has a sweet flavor and a sticky, gelatinous texture when cooked. The harvest yield of sticky rice is much smaller than other white rices, and so it is more expensive and used in Vietnam for

Mai with a selection of rice noodles.

A market stall selling three kinds of fish sauce, soy sauce, rice wine, tamarind, bean sprouts, water chestnuts, bamboo, white corn, rice flour, olives, and other fruits and flavorings.

special occasions such as New Year, weddings or worshipping ancestors. It is used both for desserts and for a side dish with meats and vegetables. **Black rice** is a decorative, sweet rice used in salads. **Wild rice** is infrequently used in Vietnamese cooking, primarily in casseroles, because it does not absorb the cooking flavors as well as cultivated rice.

Rice Flour: Flour used in Vietnamese pancakes, available frozen.

Rice Papers: Round or triangular, brittle wrappers used for spring rolls. They soften in warm water and absorb little or no oil in cooking. It takes a little practice, however, to fold and wrap them without puncturing. To buy the rice papers, Mai recommends reading all the ingredients on the package

and buying papers that do not contain tapioca.

Rice Vinegar: A clear vinegar, made from rice.

Rice Wine: A clear, mild, cooking wine made from rice.

Rau Ram: A bitter but distinctive flavored herb with a long, slender leaf that is sometimes used instead of basil or cilantro for a more subtle flavor.